Lessons
I Learned
in the
Light

JENNIFER ROTHSCHILD

Multnomah® Publishers, *Sisters, Oregon*

LESSONS I LEARNED IN THE LIGHT
published by Multnomah Publishers, Inc.
© 2006 by Jennifer Rothschild

International Standard Book Number: 1-59052-656-2

Cover photo by Randy Bacon
Interior design and typeset by Katherine Lloyd, The DESK

Multnomah is a trademark of Multnomah Publishers, Inc.,
and is registered in the U.S. Patent and Trademark Office.
The colophon is a trademark of Multnomah Publishers, Inc.
Printed in the United States of America

For information:
MULTNOMAH PUBLISHERS, INC.
601 N LARCH STREET · SISTERS, OREGON 97759
Library of Congress Cataloging-in-Publication Data
Rothschild, Jennifer.
Lessons I learned in the light : all you need to thrive in a dark world / Jennifer
Rothschild.
 p. cm.
Includes bibliographical references.
ISBN 1-59052-656-2
1. Christian life. I. Title.
BV4501.3.R68 2006
277.3′082092--dc22
                                        2006005475
06 07 08 09 10—10 9 8 7 6 5 4 3 2 1 0

"One of my favorite things about the apostle Paul is the way he always shows us his hand. 'Not that I have already obtained all this, or have already been made perfect, but I press on...' (Philippians 3:12). Jennifer Rothschild teaches in the same way, using her life as a sincere and transparent example of what it means to press toward the goal—to live a thriving, courageous life in Christ."

—SARA GROVES
SINGER/SONGWRITER

"I love Jennifer Rothschild. I've not known her long, but it doesn't take long to see her as she really is: gifted, creative, insightful, charming, and full of the love of God. She shows how to see with new and different eyes. She walks in the light and takes us with her on that journey—in life and in her book."

—MARY GRAHAM
PRESIDENT, WOMEN OF FAITH

"Like the Renaissance artists of old, Jennifer Rothschild sees with her heart. Through self-discipline, acute observation, and Christ centeredness, the tapestry of her life has been woven together by an unshakable faith. I recognized this in Jennifer long before I read her book, but now even more so. Each story reflects a woman who not only teaches us how to live in the Light but how to trust the One who is our true vision."

—LUCI SWINDOLL
AUTHOR AND SPEAKER, WOMEN OF FAITH

"Jennifer writes with transparency and depth, weaving daily life lessons with firsthand spiritual truths. Where *Lessons I Learned in the Dark* covers our life by faith rather than sight, this sequel reminds us that we can bask in God's light—light that convicts of sin, but also frees us as we realize we are known by the Father of lights. This book is a must read!"

—DR. LORI SALIERNO
PRESIDENT AND CEO, CELEBRATE LIFE INTERNATIONAL

"Sit down to a cup of coffee and delightful conversation with Jennifer Rothschild. You will see truth clearly from God's Word, wrapped in beautiful life stories. You will laugh through tears as the Spirit's voice speaks through Jennifer's honest and open walk with God."

—ESTHER BURROUGHS
ESTHER BURROUGHS MINISTRIES, BIRMINGHAM, ALABAMA

"I'm a comedian. I love to laugh. But I have also experienced dark times. After reading Jennifer's book, I found myself humming the children's song, This Little Light of Mine. Humming in the dark? Yes! And there is no one more perfect to lead us out of the darkness than Jennifer Rothschild. Hold on to the rope, kids! It's time for recess!"

—CHONDA PIERCE
COMEDIAN, INO RECORDS

DEDICATION

To Karen True
Because she loves and shines the Light.
No one could have a better friend.

CONTENTS

ACKNOWLEDGMENTS

To my husband, Phil. You are my partner in life and ministry. I love you.

To my editor, Larry Libby. You are my faithful friend and scribe. Thank you, my brother. Wasn't this fun?

To my son, Clay. I am proud to be your mom. Always cling to the Word, and the Lord will bring about great victories in your life.

To my son, Connor. While I wrote this book, you asked Jesus into your heart. May you always walk in the light of His Word.

To my writing and research assistant, Karen True. This book and this author are both the better for your wise and faithful offerings.

To my pastor, Dr. John Marshall. Thank you for your diligent and skilled handling of the Word. I am deeper and richer for it.

To my assistant, Kathryn McCall. Thank you for your tireless, loyal work and friendship.

To the Multnomah team. It was a privilege to partner with you. Thanks for being such good stewards of my message.

To Mom and Dad, Lawson and Judith Jolly. I am one lucky girl to have you. Thank you for shining the Light.

To Father God, who is my Light. How could I live without Your Word? Let it bring life to the readers of this book.

FOREWORD

Have you ever met someone and known instantly that the two of you would always be friends? That's how I felt about Jennifer Rothschild.

Of course, I can't imagine *anyone* not being drawn to this bundle of inspiration. If this book is your first introduction to Jennifer, let me give you a heads-up on what to expect.

First off, Jennifer is one of those rare individuals who is both honest *and* kind. She is delightfully candid while being tenderly aware of human frailty. I like that. I want to know the truth, but my experience has been that bottom-line frankness can loosen molars and separate friends.

But Jennifer has the ability to speak words into our lives that fit inside us as though we've been waiting a long time to hear them. They settle in like friends and they make sense. And gratefully, she's willing to open up her own humanity to make us more comfortable with ours. How hospitable. How vulnerable.

Jennifer's petite size and her darling ways may cause you to initially underestimate her, but trust me—she is one savvy gal. She is studied and current; she is relevant and well established in the Scriptures. I appreciate that.

Oh, and did I mention that Jennifer's blind? I almost forgot, because she so sees women for who they are and who they can become that her lack of physical sight is a non-issue

LESSONS I LEARNED IN THE LIGHT

for her audiences. And because Jennifer's perspective is so visionary and passionate, her sharing is as if someone finally opened a window and turned on a light in the cellar of our souls.

You'll instantly learn in Jennifer's presence that faith is her top priority, followed quickly by her love for and devotion for her husband and sons. And to watch their admiration of her is downright moving.

Don't get me wrong. I'm not trying to paint a perfect picture of Jennifer and her life. She struggles, she stumbles, and she suffers.

You will hear and see it in the pages ahead. But I want you to know that up close and personal, I find her stunning. Her faith is sterling, her commitment to her family is constant, and her determination to pass along to us the best of what she's learned is impressive.

But wait. I can't leave out the quality that captures my applause regularly when I'm with Jennifer: courage. She is one tenacious lady. But you'll figure that out in chapter 1, when you join her and her oldest son at an amusement park on a ride called The Accelerator.

I first experienced Jennifer's steady confidence at a Women of Faith conference when she was the featured speaker. Phil, her husband, escorted her on stage and left Jennifer on her own.

Picture a large, round stage, an audience of seventeen thousand, four cameras, no cane—and she can't see. Honey, she breezed around that stage like a sighted veteran using a network of carpets to alert her feet as to her whereabouts. It was fascinating. She spoke with the confidence of a lion and the gentle and playful heart of a kitten. I was mesmerized by her myriad gifts. Did I mention she sings beautifully as well?

If anyone's keeping score, I'm not certain it's fair that God has packaged so much in one vessel. Yet I, for one, don't want to miss one word that comes out of her lips and through her pen. I'm definitely a fan, and I believe you will be too. So cozy into your favorite reading place and prepare to be blessed.

Patsy Clairmont, author of *All Cracked Up: Experiencing God in the Broken Places*

INTRODUCTION

As I tucked our son Connor, who was three at the time, into bed one crisp fall night, he interrupted the routine with a challenging series of questions.

I'm used to this.

He's old enough to understand the art of stalling. It's usually executed with, "I need some water," skillfully followed by a well-timed, "I need to go potty!" When those pressing needs have been met, he may try a new tack:

"I'm scared."

"Lay down with me."

"Turn on the lamp."

"Crack open the door."

On this particular night, however, he brought out a previously untested weapon from his arsenal: three-year-old theology.

"Mommy," he asked, "does God smile like a frog or like a grandpa?"

That one stopped me in my tracks for a moment. Recovering, I told Connor that God could never look like a frog, so He must smile like a grandpa.

Then he asked, "What does God look like, anyway?"

I answered as best as I knew how, remembering 1 John 1:5: "God is Light, and in Him there is no darkness at all."

"Connor," I said, "as far as I know from the Bible, He looks like light."

Little did I know that I had just drawn the line in the sand. And so the litany of questions began.

"What kind of light, Mommy? Is He like the big, bright light in the kitchen that I like to dance under? Or is God like the lamp by the couch that's warm and snuggly?"

"I don't really know, Connor. All I know is that He's just big, beautiful, and bright!"

"Well, I like the kitchen light," he said, "because it's fun to dance under. But I like the couch lamp because it's yellow and warm."

I've found the best way to end the stalling game is to say, "Let's pray." So, we did. The day ended with an "amen" in unison and a sweet voice lifting up an "I love you, Mommy."

I went immediately into the kitchen and stood thoughtfully under the light. *Connor's right*, I thought to myself, doing a few dance steps across the tiles. *It is fun to dance here.* Moments later I walked to the couch and settled by the lamp with some hot tea. *It is warm and yellow*, I smiled.

How correct my little Connor was that night. Light can be comforting. Light can be clarifying. When I think about it, light can also be challenging. It warms us, guides us, calls us to leave our darkness, encourages us to persevere.

No wonder the psalmist compared God's Word to light in Psalm 119:105: "Your word is a lamp to my feet and a light for my path."

Perhaps the main reason the psalmist called God's Word light is because our world is dark. That's true of human beings, too. Without God in our lives, we can become very, very dark.

Paul put it this way: "For you were formerly darkness,

but now you are Light in the Lord" (Ephesians 5:8, NASB). What a statement. He isn't just saying you were in the darkness; you were the darkness.

Jesus shows us what a person in darkness is like. "But if anyone walks in the night, he stumbles, because the light is not in him" (John 11:10, NASB). "He who walks in the darkness does not know where he goes" (John 12:35, NASB).

In Romans 1:21 and Ephesians 4:18, Paul shows the impact of our darkness. Darkness involves futility of thinking, being darkened in understanding, exclusion from the life of God, and ignorance. No matter what you might think about philosophy, psychology, or higher education, none of these things can bring a human soul out of darkness. How about therapy? Self-actualization?

No, of course not.

The only remedy for darkness is light.

God's written Word is light. The psalmist declared, "The unfolding of Your words gives light; it gives understanding to the simple" (Psalm 119:130, NASB).

Just as a white cane guides me in my physical darkness, God's light guides me out of my spiritual darkness. God's light brings understanding, illumination, revelation, and gives direction.

I remember the Labor Day weekend I spent in Athens, Georgia, with my precious friend Katharyn. I love to visit her because she and her family are all treasured friends, and we have a blast when we're together. It had been a few years since my last visit and boy, had things changed. Katharyn had been busy redecorating her home and rearranging furniture.

It was nothing at all like I remembered it.

And for me, that's a big problem.

The piano was in a different room, couches were against new walls, and in some places there was new furniture that I was not yet acquainted with. Now, all of this only really matters because I can't see. I had a good mental map from previous visits, and now it was completely obsolete. The last few times I visited I enjoyed some independence, since I was so familiar with my surroundings. But this time, I realized pretty fast that I would have to pull out my cane to navigate all the new additions and changes.

I must admit, I don't really like to use my cane if I don't have to. But it was completely necessary that weekend.

I may not really like using my cane, but Katharyn's kids sure like it. Her daughter, Anya, was especially curious and it was all she could do to keep her little hands off of it.

One Sunday morning I sat down at the piano, resting my cane on the bench next to me. Anya made her way to my side and gently moved the cane so she could sit down. She held the cane in her hands, twirling it, pointing it, and thoroughly examining it. I could tell she was contemplating something.

Finally, she asked, "Are you ever embarrassed to carry your cane?"

I stopped playing to answer her sincere question.

"I used to be," I said. "Now I sometimes feel self-conscious, but I'm not embarrassed." I continued to explain. "To me, you see, my cane is my ticket to freedom. If I didn't depend on my cane, I wouldn't get to navigate or enjoy my world."

Anya was satisfied with my simple answer and left the room to play outside. But I couldn't stop thinking about what my cane represented to me—and what would happen if I refused to use it.

If I refused dependency, I would reject liberty.

In other words, because I choose to be dependent on my cane, I experience a kind of liberating independence.

It's a good picture, I think, of how we relate to Scripture. When we choose to be totally dependent on God's Word, it ushers in a freedom that we would never experience otherwise. When we rely on His wisdom and hold onto His precepts, we walk in freedom, not fear. When we fully lean on the promises in His Word, we find that we are freed from the wishing and worrying that so imprison us. The light of God's Word brings a brightness that allows us to dance. It makes clear that which could be fuzzy and dim.

Let's face it, life changes. Things are not always as we remember them. Loss happens, people we love leave, our inner worlds can get rearranged due to emotional changes. Sometimes the shadows of heartache overwhelm us and we just want to quit. We want to navigate and enjoy our world, but the only way is through dependence on a higher source of wisdom. Pure, utter dependence on God's Word truly liberates us.

God's light really is a clarifying beam that we can depend upon. And God's Word is light—a light that brings such freedom and joy that we really can dance.

God's light is warm. It comforts me and adds a sweet illumination to my darkness that is often more felt than seen.

God's light challenges me to be awake, aware, alert, careful, and ready to seize every opportunity He brings across my path.

God's light gives me the strength to stay in the race, even when I am weary. It encourages me to keep holding on, to keep moving forward, to keep reaching for His highest and best intentions for my life, no matter what my life circumstances.

It has been the light of God's Word that has compelled me to keep running my race with endurance, even in blindness. And I know that His Word will not return void in your life, either.

I love His light.

After all these years of walking in its illumination, my world would be a dark and desolate place apart from the warmth and freedom His Word gives. I'm pretty sure that when I see God someday, His smile will be that of a loving and kind Father. And our heavenly home will need no other light, because the light of the Lamb will shine there forever. Until then, I walk in the Light, learn from the Light, and depend fully on the Light to guide me home.

My friend, in the following pages you will be encouraged, equipped, and inspired from the lessons I've learned in the Light. I know they will bring you comfort, bring clarity to your path, and challenge you to never, never, never quit.

"The entrance of Your words gives light" (Psalm 119:130, NKJV).

CHAPTER ONE

Cling to His Word

They called it "The Accelerator."

For good reason.

Launching into the night sky, screams piercing the air in its wake, the great mechanical contrivance sent a surge of fear through my whole body. Just standing near it made my heart pound. And within mere moments, I would make its intimate acquaintance.

This wasn't the first time I've been stretched in such a way. In my attempts to relate to my teenage son, I have on several occasions ventured beyond the boundaries of sense and prudence.

One such excursion occurred the summer before Clayton's

sophomore year of high school. On a balmy August evening, our little family ambled through Celebration City, a theme park in Branson, Missouri. I held Phil's hand, giggled at a clown having some fun with six-year-old Connor, and sipped on my ice-cold Coke.

The night was dreamy. We were finally taking a badly needed family vacation, and my neck and shoulders felt more relaxed than they had in months. (But not for long, as it turned out). The fragrance of kettle corn and cotton candy mingled with music from the seventies and eighties, blaring from speakers throughout the park.

I found myself reminiscing to the sounds of "Dream Weaver" and singing along to "Saturday in the Park" when my perfect, relaxed mood was interrupted by Clayton's grip on my arm.

"Mom, go with me on that ride!"

"Which ride?" I asked.

Phil's slow, painful moan should have clued me in that I would not like the answer I was about to hear. My guys had stopped and were staring in awe at some midway monstrosity. Suddenly, it blasted off directly in front of us, the ground vibrating beneath our feet. I could hear the ride's quick ascent and felt the gust of wind in its wake.

And then came the screams.

I know my sounds, and I knew those riders weren't faking it. They were genuinely terrified.

"No way!" I said.

"Aw, c'mon, Mom," Clayton pleaded. "It's safe."

By this time, Phil was laughing. Little Connor emitted a

series of gasps and sighs as he watched the ride rocket abruptly heavenward, only to hurtle back toward terra firma.

"Mom?"

Okay, now I was in a real dilemma. My teenage son rarely requested my company (especially in public places)—in fact, I had the impression he didn't think hanging out with Mom was cool. And now...he wanted me to go with him. Not his dad...*me*. I felt a momentary elation that he at least thought I was cool enough to join him on a ride reserved only for the brave hearted.

The ride launched again, thundering off into what seemed to be the stratosphere. How high did that thing go? And what was a mom to do?

I knew that the more I thought about it, the more paralyzed I would become. So, feigning enthusiasm, I stepped forward, swallowed hard, and said, "Let's go!"

Phil whooped and cheered at my bravery. Then again, maybe he was celebrating the fact that it wasn't him who was about to lose his barbecue high over Branson.

Taking our place in line, I held my cane prominently in front of me. There was always the chance that the attendant would regretfully inform me that middle-aged blind women were not allowed on this ride. Then I would not only be spared the experience, but I would still collect the credit for my bravery.

No such luck.

We made it to the front of the line and were ushered to our seats. The Accelerator, I found out later, towers eighty feet in the air. It launches you suddenly into the sky before plunging you back down with back-to-back positive and negative G-forces. When the young man assisting me told me to remove my shoes so they wouldn't fly off, my breathing became shallow. What had I gotten myself into? I was already beginning to panic, and we hadn't even left the ground.

I learned later that the ride was circular in shape, and that all twelve riders were strapped in, facing out around the perimeter of the circle. At the time, however, without the benefit of sight, I really had no idea what I had so impulsively agreed to.

A cage-like set of two bars automatically lowered in front of me, and a set of belts fell down around my shoulders. The attendant helped me buckle in.

"Do you have any idea how *high* this goes?" he asked me with a chuckle. "Hey, if you're blind, maybe it's easier."

"Agghhh!" I shrieked.

"Mom," Clayton said calmly, "the ride hasn't even started yet."

I felt my "coolness" rating plummeting along with my valor.

Then the ride attendant gave instructions: "Everyone lift your hands in the air before we lift off. This helps you to relax."

I had no sooner obeyed that command than The Accelerator jerked us vertically at warp speed—and then dropped us like a stone. I screamed loudly. I mean, *really* loudly. Seizing the bars in front of me instinctively, I clung with all my strength, my hands becoming one with the metal. I held on so tight that my fingers hurt—just before they went numb.

After we landed for the final time, the attendant came to help release me from the harness. "How was it?" he asked, unfastening the buckle. He must have enjoyed the expression on my face; I could sense him trying to hold back his laughter.

I don't even know what I said in response. I was too busy catching my breath and thanking the good Lord that I was still alive.

After a brief hesitation, the attendant finally said, "Uh, ma'am? You need to let go of the bars so I can get you out."

My son was so embarrassed that he may not ever invite me to join him on a ride again.

Which is more than fine with me.

CLING

There are some things in life worth clinging to. And there are some times in life when all we can do is cling. Life has a way of presenting us with abrupt changes. Often, we can't tell whether we are being pulled up or down. Sometimes we just feel strapped, confined, and totally out of control. That's when we must cling.

Not long ago, I rediscovered a story in the Old Testament about a man who knew how to cling.

Boy, did he ever.

Eleazar was one of King David's mighty men...one of his three choicest warriors. Scripture tells the story of Eleazar's role in an amazing battle with the Philistines.

One time when the Philistines were at war with Israel, [Eleazar] and David dared the Philistines to fight them. Every one of the Israelite soldiers turned and ran, except Eleazar. He killed Philistines until his hand was cramped, and he couldn't let go of his sword. When Eleazar finished, all the Israelite troops had to do was come back and take the enemies' weapons and armor. The LORD gave Israel a great victory that day. (2 Samuel 23:9–10, CEV)

The Philistines had been Israel's nemesis for generations—a thorn in the side of God's people. Time and again through the years, they had raided and harassed the towns and villages of Israel, spilling the blood of countless young Israelite soldiers.

On this particular day, the enemy seemed unbeatable. Overpowering. They were so intimidating that the Israelite army turned tail and ran.

All but one.

The Bible says that one soldier refused to retreat. Eleazar. He stood his ground, clung to his sword, and fought like a one-man wrecking crew. One translation says he "struck the Philistines until his hand was weary and clung to the sword."

The enemy came in like a flood, and Eleazar didn't flinch. How did he prevail? The sword. He clung to the sword with such dedication, such desperation, such determination that his fingers actually "froze" around its hilt.

Can you see that in your mind's eye? The returning soldiers, probably sheepish from running away and allowing their comrade to stand alone, saw him standing there, maybe leaning up against a big rock, sword still in hand, surrounded by the dead.

"Eleazar," you can hear someone say gently, "you can set your sword down now. It's okay. The battle's over. You've won the day. The Lord has given you a great victory."

And Eleazar replies, "I would if I could, but...I can't let go."

I can imagine one lone soldier tentatively approaching the mighty man, kneeling before him, and then peeling each of Eleazar's cramped fingers from the hilt of his weapon. It was hard to see where Eleazar's skin ended and the sword began. He had wrapped every fiber of his being around that weapon. It was as if the two had become one, cemented together in those great moments of terror, courage, battle, and victory.

What a beautiful picture of what it means to cling.

Here's my question for you, my friend. When is the last time you clung to your sword—the Word of God—with *that* kind of desperation, that kind of determination?

The Bible calls itself a sword.

For the word of God is living and active. Sharper than any double-edged sword, it penetrates even to dividing soul and spirit, joints and marrow; it judges the thoughts and attitudes of the heart. (Hebrews 4:12)

Take the helmet of salvation, and the sword of the Spirit, which is the word of God. (Ephesians 6:17, NASB)

It is the weapon God gives us to fight our enemies, to overcome in any battle in our lives. Because of Eleazar's determination to cling to his sword, "the LORD gave Israel a great victory." And it's the same for you and me. Hold on tight to God's Word, and the Lord will enable you to prevail—to utterly defeat the forces arrayed against you.

But you have to cling. You have to stand your ground and hold onto that sword with everything you've got.

As in so many other areas of life, Jesus shows us the way.

JESUS AND THE SWORD

As much as I hate to admit it, sometimes God intends for us to face battles and endure wilderness experiences so we can learn to use the valuable weapon He has entrusted us with. This is the example that Jesus set for us. Matthew records that He was "led up by the Spirit into the wilderness to be tempted by the devil. And after He had fasted forty days and forty nights, He then became hungry" (Matthew 4:1–2, NASB).

Never doubt that when Satan and his demon army move to attack you, they pick the time and the battlefield. Have you noticed that? The attacks seem especially heavy when we're hungry, hot, tired, discouraged, depleted, or lonely. Our trials ensue just when it seems like we're least capable of handling them.

Why does God allow those dry wilderness wanderings and the ongoing battle with evil? Why doesn't He protect us from such times? The fact is, He sometimes *leads* us into such times.

Why? Because we will be weak, vulnerable, and useless kingdom soldiers if we never train with our swords.

Is there danger in these encounters? Of course there is. This is a dangerous world, and these are dangerous times. But He has given us a wondrous weapon to wield against the "father of lies." And God assures us that no temptation will come our way beyond our ability to handle it and emerge victorious. We have His word on it.

> But remember that the temptations that come into your life are no different from what others experience. And God is faithful. He will keep the temptation from becoming so strong that you can't stand up against it. When you are tempted, he will show you a way out so that you will not give in to it. (1 Corinthians 10:13, NLT)

When Jesus faced the enemy in that desolate place, He could have used any weapon at His disposal to knock him out with a humiliating defeat. Besides the fact that Jesus was God incarnate, possessing unlimited power, consider what else He had going for Him in the weapons department.

First, He was a rabbi—a religious "professional," you might say. Familiar with the Law and the Prophets, He led a tidy, good, religiously upstanding life. He could have pulled out the "religion" weapon from His arsenal during that duel in the desert. That's what we do at times. When the battle gets hot, we pull out our religious experience or our good works or our own virtue in order to deflect the enemy's attacks.

Bad idea.

Scripture says that "all our righteous acts are like filthy rags" (Isaiah 64:6). We can't fight a fierce enemy with a filthy rag, my friend—and that's what empty religion is.

Second, Jesus had a great personality. The Gospels portray Him as a kind teacher, compassionate friend, popular speaker, gentle leader, and compelling storyteller. He was obviously persuasive in His speech. Perhaps He could have convinced His enemy not to hit so hard, or to join Him in a peaceful singing of "Kumbayah." He could have pulled out the weapon of personality-plus and fought, but He didn't. Not for a moment. And neither should we.

How often do we muster all our strength and the collective attributes of our personality and try to stand against the enemy of our souls? But it won't work. We can't fight spiritual battles with weapons of the flesh. Our great personalities and charisma are not weapons; only truth is a weapon.

Jesus could have fought with any implement of war at His disposal, but He chose wisely. He engaged the enemy with the only weapon that guarantees victory: the sword of the Spirit, the Word of God.

Read the full account in the book of Matthew. Satan attacked three times from three different angles. He tried ridicule, he tried subtlety, he tried a brazen frontal assault.

And all three times Jesus countered the assaults of hell with "It is written...." The living Word of God quoted the written Word of God to beat back the enemy's attack. How can you and I do any less when it comes to our battles? "It is written" should be our weapon of choice. We should never counter the attacks with "It is my religious experience" or "It is my personality." Those weapons will always disappoint us, but God's Word never will.

If God has allowed you to be in a wilderness of trial or temptation, if you find yourself, like Eleazar, on a battle-field utterly alone, don't lose heart. Don't quit. God's Word is the weapon that will bring you victory, comfort, and provision. Cling to it, for your King considers you worthy to possess it.

SWORD OF HONOR

Along with millions of other Americans, I look forward to my favorite weekly television program: *Antique Road Show*. It's a marvelous parade of old collectibles and vintage treasures found in the attics of ordinary people. Sculptures, paintings, jewelry, and even toys make up the potpourri of antiquities that are carefully examined and exclaimed over by seasoned appraisers each week for all to see.

One night I was watching the show on location in Charlotte, North Carolina, when a certain item caught my attention. It was a sword. Normally, antique weapons don't pique my interest. But this time was different. I think it was the appraiser's reaction to what he saw that caused me to sit up and take note.

With childlike exuberance and a touch of reverence, Mr. Mitchell, the appraiser, exclaimed, "This is the most exciting military find I've ever seen come into the show." As he held the jewel-adorned heirloom, he asked its owner to explain the sword's origin.

Pleased and proud, the man told the story of a ceremonial blade that had been in his family since 1848, when it was presented to one of his ancestors, a general who fought in the Mexican War. The appraiser quickly noted that at the time of its presentation, such a sword was considered the highest honor bestowed by the United States government.

The impressive scabbard was beautifully engraved, indicating that the President himself had presented it. Because the blade bore such an inscription, the dealer placed an incredibly high value on this rare find.

I own such a sword.

No, better—infinitely better than that old piece of metal.

My sword, too, has been passed down through many generations. I'm not sure that I had really recognized that it was such a symbol of honor. I don't keep my sword in the attic, though. I hold onto it for dear life. I pick it up every day and notice its beautiful jewels.

You have the same sword. The sword you and I possess is God's Holy Word, inscribed by the very finger of God. It's filled with promises, hidden treasures, and powerful truth, making it an incredibly rare find.

What an honor that God Himself would entrust us with such an extraordinary gift. Hold your sword in high regard, for it is a reminder that God Himself holds you in high regard. If yours is in the attic, get it down, dust it off, test its edge, and examine its jewels. Feel its comforting weight in your hand. Hold it with reverence and cling to it with confidence.

Remember Eleazar, who became so attached to his sword he couldn't let it go. Don't let anyone or anything pry your fingers—or your heart—from the Word of God.

CHAPTER TWO

Say Farewell to Ducks

*I*t was the eleven o'clock worship hour, and my pastor was on a roll.

As usual, I was hanging on every word of his message. But this Sunday he was outdoing himself. Call it eloquent, call it passionate, call it anointed, call it whatever you like, but it was just about the best sermon I'd ever heard on the virtues of God's Word.

And there I was (in my usual spot in the second row), saying "Amen! Amen!" with practically every breath he took. I was in full accord with every word he spoke about the Bible and its inestimable value in our lives. After all, I spent a lot of time studying the Word. I was busy teaching it—and even writing books about all I was learning. There were moments in the message when I had to restrain myself from jumping out of my pew to stand behind the pulpit and finish the sermon for him.

He was dancing my dance, singing my song, humming my tune. Imagine my surprise when he hit a discordant note near the end of his remarks.

I had been riding along on his thought train, happy and content, and suddenly it was as if the train derailed. He spoke some words that were, to my mind, highly questionable.

He had been pleading with us as his congregation to spend daily time in God's Word. But as he was bringing his thoughts to a close, he paused for a moment and said, "Listen to me. If you're not having daily time in the Word, then you have a pride issue."

What did he just say? A pride issue? Oh, I don't think so!

The amens lifting from the second row went suddenly silent. For the first time all morning, I did not agree with my beloved pastor.

He's wrong, I thought. *I certainly have issues that keep me from daily time in the Word of God, but pride is NOT one of them.*

I quickly began my mental rebuttal. *I don't have a pride issue. I have other issues—like ministry, motherhood, and just plain hard circumstances.*

The pastor was still speaking, but I had tuned out, reviewing my "ministry issue." My life had changed since I entered full-time ministry. I had manuscript deadlines, I traveled several weekends every month—I was practically a "professional Christian"! How could he expect me to carve time out of every busy-sometimes-crazy day to spend time in the Word? It just wasn't always easy to do.

Warming to my own argument, I thought about a second issue that made setting aside time for Bible reading almost impossible: motherhood. Our little Connor was in the midst of potty training, and things were tough around my house. I was sleep deprived, frazzled, and numb from listening to endless episodes of *Barney* and *Veggie Tales*. I was a worn-out woman. Some days were so busy that I had to decide between a shower and reading the Bible. So, for the good of humanity, I showered.

You know, I mused, *it's not as easy for the rest of us as it might be for you, Pastor. We don't get paid to be a Christian like you do.*

But I wasn't done yet. I had one more issue that topped them all.

Blindness.

Yes—that's the mother of all issues. It's pretty hard to read the Bible when you can't see it. Yes, I have the Bible on CD. But if I place it in my little CD player and accidentally bump it, I can go from Matthew to Revelation in a nanosecond. Ah, yes, my cup runneth over with issues, but pride spilled out a long time ago.

I felt pretty satisfied with my list of excuses...and maybe just a little bit smug. Yes, all my ducks were in a neat row. So, continuing to ignore the sermon I now found offensive, I decided to take a closer look at my little feathered friends.

The Ministry Duck

This little ducky had neatly platted feathers and a smile plastered upon her beak. Beneath her feathered wings were her study Bible, prayer journal, worship CDs, and, of course, her Day-Planner. Her wings, in fact, were so full that they could never be lifted in praise or opened before God to receive what He might want to give her.

The Mama Duck

Another ducky waddled into view. When this mama duck saw her reflection in the pond, it wasn't nearly so polished as the ministry duck. The feathers atop her head were disheveled because she hadn't had time for a shower—and were in desperate need of a trim and a highlight. Her webbed feet hadn't had a pedicure since before her first little duckling hatched. Her eyes were bloodshot from lack of sleep since her duckling was now teething. She paddled dizzily through her day, from one end of the pond to the other, just trying to keep the family afloat. Privacy is a distant luxury for mama duck. She just can't squeeze any more time out of her day to spend alone with God.

The Blind Duck

Oh, this was a sassy one. When it was her turn to appear, she waddled up with her white cane and attitude to spare. Sauntering into the line beside mama duck, she took her place in a long, long row of duckies, extending as far as my imagination could see.

~ ~ ~

What a lovely set of excuses. No one could ever shoot them down. They were so innocent, so sincere, so full of worthwhile pursuits, and swimming in a stream of service to others.

Then it happened. *Bam! Bam!* Duck hunting season began.

Just as I tuned back in for my pastor's final words, he shot right through my thoughts and sent my feathered excuses flying.

"I call this a pride issue," he was saying, "because at the core of your neglect of the Word is the belief that *you really don't need God.*"

His aim was perfect, knocking all three lame-ducks right out of the sky. Unable to fly against the truth, my duckies were down to stay. He was right. Neglecting my time in God's Word—whatever my excuse—was like telling Jesus I really didn't need Him.

Terrible thought. I knew better...didn't I? I *did* need Him. I will *always* need Him. As I examined my heart, I readily affirmed that I could never navigate life on my own. And didn't want to! So why was I so smugly acting as if I could?

Resuming my internal dialogue, I told myself *It's high time you started acting on what you believe, girl. You don't have ministry issues, motherhood issues, or even blind issues. You have one issue...pride.*

I had been wounded that day for sure, but it was the right kind of wound. One that would lead me to wholeness.

We all have "issues," don't we? You've got ducks, I've got ducks, all God's children got ducks. Your ducks are any excuses that you allow to keep you from the one thing you most desperately need in life.

How many ducks have you lined up? Are your excuses really worth more to you than God's Word? Nothing has really changed in my life. I still face ministry pressures, responsibilities as a wife and mom, and yes, I am still blind. But instead of allowing those life issues to become road-blocks keeping me from my time with God and His Word, I want them to become pathways to His presence. Reminders of my profound, constant, moment-by-moment need.

We should never allow the demands of life—which admittedly seem so urgent at the time—to keep us from what is the most important. In fact, the demands of life that seem so quickly overwhelming should push us right into His arms.

Which ducks are quacking up your schedule, and keeping you from your time with God? I have found that no matter how much we love the Bible, it still takes discipline to be in the Word every day.

INDEFATIGABLE DISCIPLINE?

Clayton groaned after dinner as his dad pulled a familiar book off the kitchen shelf. "Not again," he moaned. "Why do we need to read this every night?"

"Well," Phil said simply, "you never know when you might need to know these."

The book which drew such protest from our high school freshman is *100 Words Every High School Graduate Should Know*. And even though Clayton was a few years away from graduation, we pulled out the book each night following dinner and tried to guess definitions. His dad and I think it is fun and stimulating; Clayton, on the other hand, thinks it's the very essence of cruel and unusual punishment.

Last night, for instance, we learned what it meant to be *feckless*. Perhaps you know someone who meets the qualifications. The word means lacking purpose or vitality, feeble or ineffective, careless and irresponsible. What a great adjective. But what an awful label to wear through life.

We recently unearthed a buried treasure in the word *bellicose*. Even though the word sounds so beautiful and kind of rolls off the tongue, it actually means warlike or hostile. I'm not sure about Clayton, but I still remember wonderful words from weeks ago...words like *enervated* or *indefatigable*.

Now there's a mouthful. The first means to be drained of energy and the latter means to be tireless. Aren't words magnificent, grand, spectacular, and sublime?

Lover of words that I am, I do understand my young son's antipathy (there's another gem) toward learning new terms. It takes discipline to grow a vocabulary, and discipline is neither natural nor easy.

I understand because I have felt that way about investing regular time in the Word each day. It takes discipline to grow a spiritual vocabulary filled with memorized truth.

I guess that's why it's so easy to allow the merely urgent in my life to crowd out the truly important. When it comes right down to it, I don't like discipline any more than my son Clayton does. But I'm learning something I pray that he learns in the coming days: Discipline will always lead to delight, and delight will always lead to desire. Did you get that? If you and I dedicate ourselves to the Word, discipline ourselves to read and memorize it, then we can expect the fruit of that discipline to bring us delight.

And don't we desire those things in which we delight?

The prophet Jeremiah experienced the delight and desire of God's Word. He wrote, "Your words were found and I ate them, and Your words became for me a joy and the delight of my heart" (Jeremiah 15:16, NASB).

Sometimes we moan when it comes to discipline. In fact, we become downright feckless and enervated. But be indefatigable and pick up the Book each day and night and learn something from His Word. One day you will realize that what began as discipline has now become pure, perfect, genuine, absolute, complete delight.

Listen to how a simple shepherd boy named David tried to wrap words around his elation.

The precepts of the LORD are right,
rejoicing the heart;
the commandment of the LORD is pure,
enlightening the eyes;
the fear of the LORD is clean,
enduring forever;
the rules of the LORD are true,
and righteous altogether.
More to be desired are they than gold,
even much fine gold;
sweeter also than honey
and drippings of the honeycomb.
Moreover, by them is your servant warned;
in keeping them there is great reward.
(Psalm 19:8–11, ESV)

Yes, it's a beautiful psalm, and most of us would nod our heads and say, "How true. How true." But if I can become very personal for a moment—almost more personal than I want to be—I'd like you to think what your life would be like if you could never, for the rest of your life, read a Bible at all.

IN ONE MOMENT OF SIGHT

In an interview not long ago, I was asked, "If you could see just one thing for one moment what would it be?"

The question took me aback. I really hadn't been expecting her to surface the subject at all—I have so many other things I'd rather talk about than my blindness. But since she asked, I paused for a moment to consider an answer.

After a few seconds I said, "I'd reject the offer. To me, it would be like Lay's Potato Chips. You can't eat just one!"

The interviewer laughed as I continued. "Truly, I would hesitate to choose one thing because—I'd be so afraid of later regretting my choice. I'd fear that a moment of sight might awaken something within me that has long been at rest under the blanket of contentment. I'd be afraid to arouse the desire to see."

The interviewer gave a long, contemplative sigh and moved to the next question.

Hours and even days later, however, the question haunted me. It nagged at me and began to erode what I thought had been a secure fortress of contentment. Part of the problem was that she had hit me with that question during a season of what I call "life fatigue." Ever felt like that? Just worn out by life.

I was tired of being blind. I guess that's why the question unsettled me. It felt like the sting of a bandage being torn away too quickly. I didn't *want* to be able to see for "a moment." I wanted to see for a lifetime.

Even so, it perplexed and frustrated me that I couldn't come up with an answer to her question. *If I could see for just a moment, what would I choose to see?* In spite of myself, I began to catalog all the things I might choose.

My parents' faces. *They were so young when I last saw them. What a joy it would be to see how they have aged in grace and beauty.*

My own children. *What would it be like to see their faces? What a gift that would be.*

My husband. *He was such a good-looking young man when we married. How do I know he was good-looking? He told me.*

Sunsets. *When I was a girl growing up in Miami, I saw some amazing displays at the beach. Oh, to see the ocean, or a sunset, or a seashell.*

I continued to ponder the array of possibilities, but no thought brought satisfaction. Then, at last, my discontent gave way to peace as I thought of the one thing I would choose.

If I could see for just one moment, I would open a Bible and look upon Psalm 63.

O God, You are my God; I shall seek You earnestly;
My soul thirsts for You, my flesh yearns for You,
In a dry and weary land where there is no water.
Thus I have seen You in the sanctuary,
To see Your power and Your glory.
Because Your lovingkindness is better than life,
My lips will praise You.

So I will bless You as long as I live;
I will lift up my hands in Your name. (vv.1–4, NASB)

Surprised by my choice?

Oh, my friend, how do I explain this to you?

Even as I write these words I am overwhelmed by the thought of actually seeing those eternal words. Why? Because His lovingkindness truly is better than life, better than sight, better than anything. Nothing in my life has been better to me than His lovingkindness. And I have experienced His lovingkindness from reading His Word.

I am convinced that nothing else would be worthy of my momentary gaze.

I don't want to over-spiritualize or be dramatic. It's just that the depth of emotion I feel about this makes it hard for me to put it into words.

I can understand that my choice might seem strange to you. After all, I can still access the Word because of my computer and CDs. I can listen to it being beautifully read by actors, I can hear it read by my children, my husband, and my pastor. So why would I want to use the only moment of sight to see something I can hear anytime?

I know that God's Word is much more than written words on a page.

It's much more than ink on India paper. But there's just something about the *Book*...that's how I used to experience the Word. And no longer can.

Do you realize what a privilege it is to be able to pick up your Bible and open its pages to read *anytime you want to?* It's a liberty that you may not realize until it's lost. It's a comfort that you can't fully appreciate or understand unless the privilege has been removed.

I have never seen the faces of my boys or my husband, so I don't feel the loss in the same way. But I did see my Bible. My eyes lingered on its pages from early childhood. As a young girl, I remember my red leather Bible that I read on my own out of curiosity and even childlike desire. As a young teen curled up in my bed in Miami—unsure of myself, insecure, afraid—I would read my Bible late into the night.

It was mine. I underlined it. I marked the pages. I held it. Even though it was merely ink on paper wrapped in a leather binding, it represented something physical and tangible. And to hold it again and see it...would be to experience it in a way that was precious to me, and in a way to which little else compares. It was a privilege to see it with my own eyes. I wish I had taken even more advantage of that privilege. Now, it's gone. And I miss it.

I loved my Bible so much that even years after the onset of my blindness, I still carried it to church with me. Holding the book, smelling the leather, hearing the thin rustle of the pages was to me a bit of security—like holding hands with heaven. But I finally stopped doing even that, because of the curious questions.

Even now, when I am with my precious friend and writing assistant Karen, I feel a tinge of jealousy and long to be able to pick up the Word and read it like she does. Her Bible is well worn, and she has her history marked and jotted in the margins. She loves the Word and she treats her Bible accordingly.

I envy that. I would love that. I miss that.

Oh, my friend, of course I would love to see the precious faces and sunsets and magnolias, but I know they will all eventually fade. After all, the flowers faded a long time ago in my world. The grass does wither, as the apostle Peter put it, and faces age and change. Flowers wilt away; sunsets wane. But the Word...it's the same—just as glorious on earth as it will be in heaven. God's Word will never fade, wither, or return void.

To see the Scripture is a foretaste and a settling reminder of what is truly, eternally mine. The Word was my love before my kids were born, and the Word will be my love after my husband and parents go home to heaven. It's my companion. It's forever reliable; I am dependent on it.

Right now, in faith, I cling to the Word as I receive it, but I long for the day when my faith becomes sight.

I know I will see my kids' faces in heaven. In fact, I can't wait. I know I will see my parents—overflowing with life. My memory of an earthly sunset will be dull and colorless compared to the vibrant, transcendent glories of heaven.

If only given a moment of sight, how could I really choose a sure thing? How could I really make a choice I would never regret? Seems like the Bible is the only choice I could make that wouldn't disappoint me. A choice I could never regret. I would be able to hang onto that memory as a beautiful piece of my past and a joyous foretaste of my future.

And so, farewell to ducks. They are no longer welcome to waddle into my world. How could I have ever allowed my ducks to keep me from the discipline of a daily time in the

Bible? How could I neglect my exposure to the light of God's Word when it is the only light I really have? His Word is worthy of my discipline; it is worthy of my devotion. And it is worthy of yours.

Your eyes may see sunsets and faces. Your eyes may squint at the brightness of a steamy summer day, but you still need light. Deeper light. A light so radiant it touches blind eyes and pushes aside the shadow of death. It is the light of His Word that really allows you to see, to run, to grow, to finish strong.

David wrote: "For with You is the fountain of life; In Your light we see light" (Psalm 36:9, NASB).

Nothing else comforts me, guides me, and illuminates my darkness like the light of His Word as the Holy Spirit opens it to my understanding. It is His Word alone that compels me to keep on running the race even when I am fatigued by life. Even when loss stuns me and scrapes against the bottom of my soul, it is the Word that I run to so I can make sense of it all.

That, my friend, is desire.

When we discipline ourselves in the Word, it will lead to delight. And delight will always lead to desire. To long for the Word more than we long for life is to never be disappointed.

CHAPTER THREE

Be a Risk Taker

Most of us approach hot dogs with a pretty traditional mindset. We slip it neatly in a bun, douse it with ketchup and mustard, and then top it off with sweet pickle relish. Some of the more adventurous among us cloak the mystery meat in chili or layer it over with sauerkraut.

When I was pregnant with both our sons, I actually craved hot dogs. I couldn't get enough of them, personally downing a minimum of a pack a week. For all my experience with the fabulous franks, however, I apparently completely missed out on the *right* way to eat them.

Yesterday, as I placed Connor's lunch before him, I told him that he needed to eat his hot dog and carrots, and then he could have some strawberries and whipped cream. As motivation, I set the plate of strawberries and the bowl of whipped cream on the table above his plate.

The strategy was apparently working. My little guy began to rapidly consume his hot dog, proclaiming that it was the best he'd ever had.

I finally figured out why his ordinary dog was so delicious. He was doing something only a four-year-old would do: dipping every bite into the whipped cream. He offered me a taste of this new culinary sensation, and I casually declined, trying not to gag.

My point is twofold. First, never dip your strawberries in whipped cream which has once belonged to a four-year-old hot dog connoisseur. Second, we must all learn to think outside the bun. According to Connor, if you don't put whipped cream on your hot dog it will taste "plain." And he let me know that he was *really* tired of plain hot dogs.

Sometimes our lives are simply plain, and we can grow weary of the "same ol', same ol'."

That's not the way God would have it.

Jesus came that we might have life, and not just plain life, not just vanilla, one-size-fits-all, run-of-the-mill life, but life that is abundant.

"The thief comes only in order to steal and kill and destroy," He told a man who had sought Him out one windy night. "I came that they may have and enjoy life, and have it in abundance (to the full, till it overflows)" (John 10:10, AMP).

What are we talking about here? The kind of life that is dipped in sweetness and smothered with all the good things of God. But in order to experience all that abundant life has to offer, we may have to climb out of some completely familiar, perfectly comfortable ruts...and venture into the territory of risk.

RELUCTANCE

Christmas dinner had long since ended and we were still visiting around the table.

"Why don't we go sit in the living room?" I suggested.

My sister-in-law quipped, "Because we fear change!" We erupted in laughter over such a dramatic answer to my simple question. But there was a bit of truth in her humor.

Most of us feel a tinge of reluctance when it comes to change, because it means we must take a risk and release some of our control. Children feel it on the first day of kindergarten. Outwardly confident teens sense it when they step foot on their new high school campus. Most of us experience it on the first day of a new job. Lots of us cringe when we contemplate a new hairstyle—and our hearts race if a move is on the horizon.

But where is our spirit of adventure? Why is it that change and letting go invokes hesitation? Is it that the predictable and familiar make us feel safe? Robert Frost shaped our misgivings into a poem he called "Reluctance."

> Ah, when to the heart of man
> Was it ever less than a treason
> To go with the drift of things,
> To yield with a grace to reason,
> And bow and accept the end
> Of a love or a season?

I guess what he's saying is that we are all clingers. We wrap ourselves around what we know and love and are reluctant to release. But if we cling to God's Word, then we are more willing to take risks in this life because we realize that we were made for adventure. Jesus Himself invites us to risk our preconceived notions and our comfort, to gain the ride of a lifetime—an eternal lifetime. "For whoever wishes to save his life," He declared, "will lose it, but whoever loses his life for My sake, he is the one who will save it" (Luke 9:24, NASB).

Adventure, you see, demands that we risk letting go.

Sometimes what we attempt to hold so tightly really has a tight hold on us. Have you ever thought about that? When we try so hard to be in control, we can often find that it is our own insecurity that really controls us. An unwillingness to let go simply keeps us bound. It's only as we risk and release that we truly receive.

RISK

Sometimes I only play in the key of C, color inside the lines, and look out the window instead of going outside. You know what I mean. I have seldom jumped in the water without first sticking my toe in to check the temperature. Why do I play it safe?

I call myself an edge dweller. Do you know what that is? An edge dweller is the person who stands right at the line, peers over, analyzes the risk, wishes to jump, takes a deep breath...and turns the other way and *runs*.

The reason I like to hug the edge is because I have taken some risks in my life, and, well...sometimes they've turned out, and sometimes they haven't. Let's face it—life offers us lots of opportunities to risk. Just by rolling out of bed and putting our feet on the floor in the morning, we are invited to experience the adventure of growing, learning, failing, and myriad other thrills.

Relationships fall into that category. Every relationship is something of an adventure—because every relationship involves risk. That risk, however, carries with it magnificent rewards, even if the outcome isn't what we would have chosen.

Several years ago I took a big risk with my (now) friend Karen. I had known who she was for some time, but we had never met. At the time, I was preparing to write my first book proposal, and I needed someone to help me. I really had no idea of Karen's personality, skills, or even her interest. But I had observed her life, and felt strongly led to call her and ask her to consider joining me on the project.

To call a perfect stranger on the phone and ask her to help me do something that I wasn't even confident about launching into in the first place felt like a big risk to me. I remember psyching myself up, praying, trying to control my nervous breathing...and then dialing Karen's number.

"Hi, Karen," I said. "You don't know me. My name is Jennifer Rothschild and I am trying to write a book. I know this sounds crazy, but...I felt led to call you and ask if you would be interested in helping me?"

I will admit, I was expecting an awkward silence from Karen...followed immediately by a gracious escape from the phone call. I just knew she would hang up and immediately call her husband: "Gerry, you won't believe the weird phone call I just got. I'm afraid that wacky blind woman suffers from delusions of grandeur. Either that, or she's really needy for friends—and I'm her new target."

But none of that happened. Instead, she said, "Oh, I know who you are. That sounds so interesting. I would love to talk to you about writing a book!"

Little did I know that the nerve-racking, risky step out of my comfort zone would land me in one of the best friendships and partnerships I've ever experienced. Don't you love it when risks pay off like that? What a great reward.

But not all risks turn out roses and sunshine. Otherwise...they wouldn't be risks, would they? I took another risk within what I thought was a very secure friendship, and the reward was not what I expected.

After almost a year with a precious friend whom I will call Julie, I took a big risk and confronted her about her depression. I had watched her moods change over the many months of our friendship. I had seen her become less able to snap out of her valley times—and I knew she had once been on medication to help her with the chemical imbalance that caused her downward spirals. So one fall day as we drove to lunch, I decided that if I were really her friend, it required some truth telling.

One of the reasons it was risky for me to confront Julie was because I wasn't quite sure how she would receive my comments. I didn't want to hurt her feelings or our friend-ship. She was special to me.

But even so, it was worth the risk. *She* was worth the risk.

"Julie," I began, "I've watched you change gradually over

the last few months, and I'm concerned. I think you might need to be back on your medicine."

That was it. That was all I said. And my statement was met with silence. Cold, loud silence. As I prodded, she maintained her iceberg composure—and came up with an excuse to cancel lunch. The weeks that followed were very painful for me. Julie systematically removed me from her world. No matter how gently I questioned her, no matter how persistently I confronted what was happening, I met with a cold, unyielding brick wall.

I had taken a risk to tell her what I thought was necessary truth, and I had come up a loser. She wasn't going back on her meds, and as far as she was concerned, our friendship was over.

So was it worth the risk?

I will admit, I was plagued with questions. Did I really know her as well as I thought I did? Was I out of line to confront her?

I lost the friendship, but really, I still gained. The reward of my risk was greater wisdom, a more tender heart, and the affirmation that risk is always worthy, even when the result isn't what I would have chosen.

Years later, we reunited at a women's conference and the walls fell as the tears flowed. Restoration was the final result. Risk carries with it both the potential for great loss and great reward.

But there are no rewards apart from risk.

Are you willing to risk? A lesson I learned in the Light has helped me to be more of a risk taker. It's found in the book of Matthew.

RELEASE

Jesus addressed the potential adventurers of His day, calling them to be risk takers rather than hole makers. Well, that's not exactly what he said, but you'll see what I mean. His parable in Matthew 25:14–27 tells us a lot about ourselves. There were three servants, each given a portion of their master's money. Two were risk takers. They invested and had more to offer their master. The third, however, was a hole maker. Fearing risk, he took his portion and buried it.

The master's response to the hole maker was basically, "No risk, no return. You could have taken at least a small risk by investing. After all, the money I gave you didn't come with a shovel. It was granted to you so you could make some choices and take some chances."

Here's the way Eugene Peterson paraphrased the words of the Master in *The Message*: "That's a terrible way to live! It's criminal to live cautiously like that! If you knew I was after the best, why did you do less than the least? The least you could have done would have been to invest the sum with the bankers, where at least I would have gotten a little interest. Take the thousand and give it to the one who risked the most. And get rid of this 'play-it-safe' who won't go out on a limb" (vv. 26–28, *The Message*).

Oh, my friend, our lives were given to us so *we* would make some choices and take some chances. Are you a risk taker or a hole maker? Do you risk, release, and gain reward in spite of reluctance? Or are you an adventure avoider? Do you stand at the edge of abundant life, grasping your shovel, digging a safe place to hide? Don't trust your shovel and shallow hole more than you trust God. He is worthy of your release.

The ultimate adventure happens when we risk release—when we dare to let go. Consider what the Word tells us about those who dared to let go...or not.

THOSE WHO DARED...NOT

When the Israelites began their wilderness sojourn, God positioned them for risk taking. Actually, He provided a test to see if they viewed their trust in Him as a risk. Each day, God told Moses, the people would receive all they needed to eat. Their new delicacy was called manna. Here's what God told Moses:

> "I will rain down bread from heaven for you. The people are to go out each day and gather enough for that day. In this way I will test them and see whether they will follow my instructions." (Exodus 16:4)

There was one condition to God's provision: no hole making. "No one," He commanded, "is to keep any of it until morning" (Exodus 16:19). But some of the Israelites did not obey or trust—or whatever you want to call it. (There is rarely a separation between trusting and obeying.) Some people grasped their shovels and dug, dug, dug. Instead of doing what God said, these hole makers hid away some manna for breakfast...just in case God didn't come through the next day. They saw trusting and obeying as too big a risk.

The hole making didn't pay off though. By morning the manna had become putrid.

God chose to make the people of Israel live in daily dependence upon Him. The wilderness was provided to make risk takers out of the hole makers in the crowd. It was an opportunity for the Hebrew children to live in utter dependence on God.

Perhaps, if you find yourself in a wilderness, it's for the very same reason. So that you may "not live on bread alone, but on every word that comes from the mouth of God" (Matthew 4:4).

God allows wilderness in our lives so we can experience the liberating adventure of trust. You don't learn these things lounging by the fire in an easy chair. He expects us to walk through our dark valleys with open hands of trust and praise, rather than hands sweaty and weary from grasping our shovels.

Just to keep everything in the proper perspective, I'd like to let you in on a little secret: *We're not really in control of our lives anyway.* To acknowledge this and then step into life with confidence in a loving God is to taste the sweet, spicy, and satisfying flavors of adventure.

In our darkness, God's light guides us.

In our wilderness, God's manna feeds us.

It is no risk to trust the One who is totally trustworthy. It is no risk to place our faith in the One who is Faithful. Why cling to our shovels when we can cling to His Word? Seems to me that being a hole maker is a far greater risk than being a righteous, redeemed risk taker. Try as they might, hole makers will never find the abundant life tucked away in the back of a secure tunnel. No, life overflowing is reserved for those who cast themselves on the goodness and lovingkindness of God, refusing the temptation to hold back and self-protect.

After thinking about these hole makers, it made me want to drop my shovel and walk right off the edge of my map into unknown regions. Are you like the manna-hoarding Israelites who dared not, or are you like the risk takers below?

THOSE WHO DARED

Letting go led Abraham to risk his security and leave his country.[1]

The LORD had said to Abram, "Leave your country, your people and your father's household and go to the land I will show you".... So Abram left, as the LORD had told him. (Genesis 12:1, 4)

By faith Abraham, when called to go to a place he would later receive as his inheritance, obeyed and went, even though he did not know where he was going. (Hebrews 11:8)

When you and I think of a move, we think about pulling up stakes from one side of town and landing a few miles away. Or trading one American city for another. Or maybe leaving the Midwest for the West Coast.

When God called Abraham and Sarah to leave Ur of the Chaldees for a land He would show them, it was more like a transfer to Mars. The world was young and wide and full of mysteries and perils.

On the word of an invisible God, however, here is a couple that abandoned their home, their familiar city, their friends, their extended family, and their way of life, to start off on a journey with no map, no directions, and no stated destination.

Imagine! And please don't think of these people as super-religious, stained-glass saints. They were as real, as human, as vulnerable, and as full of fears and feelings as you. But when God called, they simply risked everything and followed.

Letting go led a reluctant Moses to risk catastrophic failure—*again.*[2]

> The LORD said, "I have indeed seen the misery of my people in Egypt. I have heard them crying out because of their slave drivers, and I am concerned about their suffering. So I have come down to rescue them from the hand of the Egyptians.... So now, go. I am sending you to Pharaoh to bring my people the Israelites out of Egypt." (Exodus 3:7–8, 10)

When you're young and you make a colossal mistake, you are sometimes allowed to "take your licks" and bounce back, fully reclaiming your life. But what if you made a huge mistake, ran to another country, gave up everything you'd ever known, and took a job as a minimum-wage laborer? *And then stayed there for forty years.*

Imagine that (if you can), and then picture yourself receiving a divine summons to return to the very scene of your terrible failure and to confront the very people who had been involved in your sudden departure. Oh...and add one more small variable: You're asked to take on the job of leader and representative of several million people.

How would you feel? Shocked? Scared? Incredulous? Insecure? Of course! But because God said so, you walk straight out of a forty-year exile and head back to the scene of your greatest defeat...in order to lay hands on what may be your greatest victory.

Letting go led Hannah to release her dream and give up her little boy, Samuel.[3]

"Sir, do you remember me?" Hannah asked. "I am the woman who stood here several years ago praying to the LORD. I asked the LORD to give me this child, and he has given me my request. Now I am giving him to the LORD, and he will belong to the LORD his whole life." (1 Samuel 1:26–28, NLT)

What woman who has yearned for years on end to cradle a baby of her own in her arms can imagine giving him away as a toddler? Hannah, who had wept before the Lord pleading for a child, had her prayers answered. But keeping the terms of her promise, she released the little boy to the Lord's service with the priest at Shiloh, believing all would be well for both her and her son.

Walking away from that worship center, leaving the desire

of her heart behind, must have been the most wrenching, heartbreaking thing she would ever do. But the Lord honored her for her faith by both richly blessing her boy and by granting her additional children—three boys and two girls.

And so it goes through Scripture. The pages of the Bible list man after man, woman after woman who—because of their faith in a faithful God—were willing to let go of what they had in order to gain what had been promised.

Young David risked his very life to challenge a blasphemous giant.[4]

At God's commands and for God's mysterious purposes, the prophet Hosea released his expectations of a happy marriage and home to marry a woman who would break his heart again and again.[5]

Peter and Andrew risked their very livelihood, released their nets, and followed Jesus.[6]

Onesimus risked punishment, reproach, and reenslavement by obediently returning to his master, Philemon.[7]

Jesus released His royal rights as God's Son, relinquished His very life, and became obedient to death on a Roman cross.[8]

And what did they receive? They received far more than they risked. They gained much more than they lost. The same odds are in your favor, my friend. There is no risk when we release our control to God. The Word tells us that "he who promised is faithful" (Hebrews 10:23).

So embrace the adventure of completely trusting Him, for He is completely trustworthy.

Trust in the LORD forever,
for the LORD, the LORD, is the Rock eternal.
(Isaiah 26:4)

The Israelites received their manna until the day they arrived in the Promised Land (Exodus 16:35). Likewise, you and I have the Bread of Life to sustain us until we reach our Promised Land. It nourishes us and equips us to trust God completely, drop our shovels, and step out in obedience. So, when you're challenged to change, when you're called to leave the old or embrace the new, when it's time to let go or step out of your comfort zone, be a risk taker. Overcome your reluctance. Drop the shovel, trust Him, and release your control to God.

Trust GOD from the bottom of your heart;
don't try to figure out everything on your own.
Listen for GOD'S voice in everything you do, every-
where you go;
he's the one who will keep you on track.
(Proverbs 3:5–6, *The Message*)

CHAPTER FOUR

Have Courage, Not Confidence

On the heels of turning forty, I ran smack into a fashion crisis.

Should I continue to wear the same style of clothing I'd worn for the past decade? Or was it time for a fresh breeze to blow through my stale wardrobe?

Well, I knew the answer to that question.

I just didn't want to face it.

The world had turned round and round, seasons had fled, and styles had changed, while the contents of my closet remained comfortably the same. I was settled into a snug, easy, but admittedly dull pattern. You know what I mean. Certain colors. Particular lines. Similar styles. But now, as I stepped into my fourth decade of life, it seemed like the right time to reassess. My hair was now a different color, and my body was hosting the latest and maybe not the greatest new lines. And the old wardrobe? Well, it needed a little lift since this new decade brought with it the tugging effects of gravity.

I needed a little spice. It was time to step out.

But it isn't that easy to simply step out of a deep rut. You have to *climb* out hand over hand. It's a major effort and investment of emotional energy.

Right at the front of my closet, I had four identical suits, all safe and traditional. I say they were identical, but in reality they were different colors. And even the colors weren't that adventurous...black, gray, brown, and, you guessed it, the ever exciting navy.

So at the urging of my most honest and loyal friends and with the full support of my family, I finally went shopping. That's when I discovered that I not only had a fashion crisis, but I also had a confidence crisis. I had no idea what to buy. I was uneasy in this venture toward a new look. I really wasn't sure of what I even liked.

I was also unsure of *how* to update my style. Remember that the last fashion I saw with my own eyes as a young teen was that of the Lady Diana Spencer before she became the Princess of Wales. So I was stuck with mental images of white stockings, linebacker-like shoulder pads, and stiff tailored suits. I also had the image of the ever-stylish Jacqueline Kennedy Onassis seared on my memory. I loved her classic look and clean lines.

These were my only points of reference, so you can imagine the building anxiety I experienced as my friends started piling clothes into the fitting room. There were tiny ruffles and bits of lace. Long shirts, short skirts, low-waisted pants, and high heeled shoes. My confidence waned with each selection I tried. The clothes my friends brought into the fitting room were cheery, bold, and colorful. As only good friends can, each reassured me that I too was cheery, bold, and colorful.

I felt very little confidence in venturing out into the world of hot pink and leather, especially when both were located on the same piece of clothing. Even so, I swallowed hard and made up my mind to be brave. Instead of gravitating to the classic Jackie O clothes that I would normally have chosen, I laid aside my insecurity and added a splash of trendy J-Lo to my wardrobe. Now I am the proud-yet-slightly-insecure owner of a pair of leather pants and a hot pink suede jacket. Whew!

In the days that followed, however, my new purchases remained neatly and safely tucked behind my closet door. Well...wasn't it daring enough just to buy them? Did I have to *wear* them, too?

What's keeping me from debuting the new look? I whined to myself. When I chose to be honest, I had to admit that a lack of confidence is what kept me from wearing them. I just didn't feel confident. If I just felt a little more confident, then I could exercise courage. Or so I thought.

After weeks of encountering my leather pants hanging in my closet, however, I decided I would not wait until I felt confident. Instead I would, at the first opportunity, slip my forty-year-old self into those sassy pants and be courageous. In other words, I would have courage even if I didn't have confidence. Think about that. Do you realize that those two concepts are often mistaken for each other?

Courage and confidence are not the same thing. Confidence is a feeling; courage is an action. Let me put it this way. In our spiritual lives, lots of us simply wait for feelings of confidence before we exercise courage. The Bible never tells us to *feel* something and then act. No, it tells us to trust Someone and then act. Rather than feeling our way into a right action, we must act our way into right feelings.

Waiting for confidence to arrive can only make us more uncertain, because when we fail to act, we lose hope. If we are to persevere through our faith walk, we must be brave even when we don't feel self-assured.

That is one of the most liberating lessons I have ever learned in the Light. The Bible demonstrates this through countless examples of those who had no confidence in the flesh, but who did what brave believers do. *They stepped out with courage—even when they lacked confidence.*

WHAT DOES GOD REQUIRE?

Do you think Abraham felt confident when he climbed Mt. Moriah with a sharp knife, a stack of firewood, and his only son—with no alternative sacrifice in sight?

Did Moses' mother feel totally confident when she laid

her sweet baby in a basket to float down the Nile?

We can all identify with how the grown-up Moses wore his own lack of confidence on his sleeve when God asked him to confront Pharaoh. He stuttered his way through all his insecurities.

I think of the woman with an issue of blood. How in the world could she have felt confident? There she was, in the middle of a crowd. She was ceremonially unclean. It would have been practically criminal for her to touch a Rabbi. She didn't reach for the hem of Jesus' garment out of a sense of confidence. No, it was courage. Pure, raw, desperate courage.

Esther didn't march boldly into King Xerxes' throne room and confidently state her case. Instead, it took the persuasive arguments of her beloved cousin Mordecai, three days of prayer and fasting, and a couple of dinners with the king before Esther could muster the courage to tell Xerxes why she had risked so much. She lacked confidence. Of course she did. I'm sure I would too if I had to stand in her slippers. But she acted with heroic courage and saved her people as a result.

God doesn't require confidence; He asks only for courage. If we wait for a feeling of confidence to settle in before we step out, we may never act. We must be willing to get out of our comfort zone and experience the uncertain adventure of exercising courage in spite of our lack of confidence. When we do, then we find that an amazing confidence results. Yes, a confidence in God and in His promises.

THREE GIFTS OF COURAGE

God did not give us the spirit of timidity or fear. Second Timothy 1:7 tells us exactly what He has given us. "For God has not given us a spirit of timidity, but of power and love and discipline" (NASB). I want you to grab hold of the three things that Paul claimed as gifts from God in this verse, because God has given us these same three gifts. These three things will bolster your courage and renew your confidence.

Power

What has God given you in place of timidity? He has given you power. Yes, He has! He said so. The Greek word for *power*, "dunamis," refers to the kind of power that exists in something or someone inherently—within its very nature. It's a power that shows itself through exertion. We get our word *dynamite* from this word. This kind of power requires our cooperation. Just as a stick of dynamite needs a touch of fire to release its great power, so it is with our will. When we recognize that God's power is our gift, we simply ignite its potential in our lives by stepping out and applying it.

Paul wrote to the church in Philippi about this kind of power when he said, "I can do all things through Christ who strengthens me" (Philippians 4:13, NKJV).

"All things" kind of power is indeed dynamite.

What are you timid about? In what areas of your life today do you lack confidence? No matter what answer pops into your mind, it falls into the "all things" category. Why? Because all things means *all things*. That means even when you don't feel confident, even when you lack courage, you can do those things...through Christ. You *do* have the power to accomplish all the things that God calls you to accomplish, and you *can* do it through Christ who is your strength. Yes! It's as true as the morning sunrise, and as near as your next heartbeat.

What intimidates you? It is no match for the power of Christ in and through you. My friend, it isn't even close.

Love

What else did God give you instead of timidity? He gave you love. The times in my life when I have been the most timid and lacking in self-confidence have been those seasons when I was least secure in my husband's love. It's not that Phil ever intentionally held back his love for me. It's just that in our mutual immaturity during the early years of our marriage, he didn't always express his love for me in a way I could readily recognize. But as the second decade of our marriage began to unfold, there was no doubt of his loyal, kind, committed love for me. It had been there all along, but after ten years, he learned how to communicate it and I learned how to recognize it.

Can I just say that the result was, and still is, wings? I am secure enough to be vulnerable, secure enough to risk, secure enough to fail. That is a result of love.

If imperfect human love can overcome the effects of timidity, how much more can the perfect love of God?

"There is no fear in love," the apostle John tells us. "But perfect love drives out fear" (1 John 4:18). The Greek word for love in both 2 Timothy 1:7 and the verse you just read is *agape*. It is the perfect, unconditional, unmerited, unreserved love of God lavished on each of us. It is not based on our deeds; neither is it awarded according to our worthiness. Agape is from God to you...just because.

How can you and I allow fear to govern us when we've received this extravagant kind of love? We should be emboldened by agape love, which says, "I love you when you fail. I love you when you succeed beyond your wildest imagination. I love you, and My love is stronger than your insecurity. My love for you is bigger than your fear, stronger than the timidity that binds you, and deeper than your deepest insecurity."

It makes me want to shout with the apostle John, "Behold what manner of love the Father has bestowed on us!" (I John 3:1, NKJV). Receive the over-the-top love of God. He longs to lavish it upon you. He wants you to have wings—and be brave enough to spread them and soar.

Self-Discipline

The third and final gift God gave you in place of your timidity is self-discipline. I remember the first time I met Beth Moore. It was in the early 1990s and I was in my late twenties. We'd both been invited to participate in a conference in south Florida.

She and I clicked from the start. I was mesmerized by her handling of the Word and thought she was absolutely genuine and loads of fun. And so I picked up the few speaking tapes she had available at her table. The message I most wanted from our weekend together was one she gave on self-control. It resonated with me, and over the years God has used it to continually teach and guide me.

Recently, as I was preparing one of my Bible studies, I retrieved my beloved tape. As I sat in a comfy chair listening to her introduction, I was struck again by the profound truth she was unfolding. Then as I continued to listen, something else struck me...*the amount of food I had consumed during her thirty-minute message.*

During the introduction, I ate a handful of dark chocolate. I actually stopped the tape mid-message to go get a cup of coffee with the nicest French vanilla cream you've ever tasted. Near the end of the tape, I found myself dropping leftover Easter jelly beans into my mouth. I did pause my indulgence a few times throughout her teaching, just long enough to record a verse...and then resumed eating.

That's when it struck me. As I listened to a message on self-control, I was myself absolutely out of control.

Second Timothy 1:7 uses the word *self-discipline*. It reminds us that we are positioned for a life of moderation, soundness of mind, and yes, self-control. The good news is that what God calls us to do, He equips us to do. In Galatians 5, one of the fruits of the Spirit that should blossom from our yielded life is none other than self-control. God knows our weaknesses, and He provides through His Spirit the self-control we need. Our part is to so walk in the Spirit, that we will fulfill the desires of the Spirit.[9]

When we have this kind of self-control (Spirit controlled self-control), it will penetrate every weakness that intimidates us. If it is our thoughts that bind us to a life of timidity, then we need to bravely proclaim that we can hold "every thought captive to the obedience of Christ" (2 Corinthians 10:5, NASB). If it is an action or addiction that intimidates us, continually overpowering our will, then we can agree with the truth that "no temptation has seized you except what is common to man. And God is faithful; he will not let you be tempted beyond what you can bear. But when you are tempted, he will also provide a way out so that you can stand up under it" (1 Corinthians 10:13).

Oh my friend, don't wait to feel confident about your ability to control all your weaknesses. Recognize that God has given you the *gift* of self-control. Be brave and exercise it. As you act with courage, watch how feelings of confidence will follow. And don't miss where your real confidence will come from. It will be a confidence in God Himself, and in His Word. The prophet Malachi reminds us that God's Word never will return void.[10] It will always accomplish what God intends. So be confident in His Word, and exercise courage.

Shortly after the explosion of the shuttle Colombia in 2003, I heard an interview on the evening news. The anchorman was questioning a former astronaut, probing the man's feelings on future space travel. The question that caught my attention went something like this: "Aren't you afraid to venture back into space? Surely your confidence in NASA has been shaken."

The astronaut's response reminded me a lot of the difference between courage and confidence, and how fear or timidity impacts the two. He solemnly answered that his fear of *not* doing it was greater than his fear of dying doing it.

In other words, the astronaut's decision to step out in courage had nothing to do with confidence. That's why fear did not impact his willingness to persevere.

I want my faith journey to be so precious to me that my fear of not pursuing will be greater than my fear of dying as I pursue. Don't you? Quitting is what I fear most, because quitting represents the ultimate death. *To finish well, we must fear quitting more than failing.* We must fear giving up more than we fear giving our all.

So don't ever let fear keep you from stepping out in courage. Don't wait for your confidence to exceed your fear. Quite honestly, that may never happen. But recognize that God didn't give you fear; He gave you love, power, and self-control.

Love will motivate your courage, power will give muscle to your courage, and self-control will help you maintain courage. Now those are some reasons to feel confident.

So, step out. Don't let a confidence crisis keep you from running your race with perseverance. After all, you are not of those who shrink back!

10:39!

I've always tried to find quick and creative ways to communicate with my sons. As a mother of two boys, I learned very long ago that their DNA does not predispose them to lengthy conversations, meaningful talks, or many words. So early on, I made a habit of simply saying "4:13!" to them.

You see, "4:13" is a reference to Philippians 4:13, the beloved Scripture I mentioned earlier: "I can do all things through Christ who strengthens me" (NKJV). So each time I yell, "4:13!" after them as they leave for school or a soccer game, they know what it means...that they can do all things as Christ gives them strength. It's a great way, in very few words, to boost their confidence.

In the last few months, however, a new phrase has replaced the "4:13" mantra.

10:39!

"But we are not of those who shrink back." Those are the first words of Hebrews 10:39. It's what the writer told the worn-out Jewish believers enduring persecution, and it's what I tell my boys. It's my way of reminding them to have courage and not give up. And it seems those eight little words are making a big impression on my five-year-old Connor.

As a type A personality, I'm ashamed to admit this, but my video cabinet is a disaster. Videos and DVDs are all mixed together, and none of them are stored in their correct cases. It's almost impossible to find what you're looking for. Connor was recently searching through this mess for one of his favorite DVDs. After about ten minutes, my little man began to lose heart, so he came and asked me for help. I began to dig through the video cabinet, pulling out empty containers and old videos. I also began to lose heart, and commented on how hard it was going to be to locate his DVD of choice.

"Mom," he announced, "we are not of those who shrink back."

"You're right, Connor," I replied, getting to my feet with a smile. "So you just keep on looking." As I took my first step toward the door little Connor yelled, "Mom! WE are not of those who shrink back! WE means both of us!"

I laughed, did a 180, and knelt again before the video cabinet. Thankfully, by some miracle, Connor instantly put his hand on the exact DVD he was looking for. "I found it! I found it!" he squealed, running to pop the disc into its player. I was relieved that the search had ended, but was grateful for what I discovered in the process—that "we" really does mean both of us.

Sometimes it's easier to have courage and persevere when you have a buddy. Every football player needs to hear the fans chant, "*We* will, *we* will, rock you!" just when he's starting to feel weak-kneed and defeated. Every kid needs a soccer mom who yells "Good try!" when the goal is elusive.

One of the most reliable companions for your journey, a companion that will always cheer you on, is God's Word. It provides all the cheers and encouragement you need to keep on stepping out in courage.

Scripture says, "For you have need of endurance, so that when you have done the will of God you may receive what is promised" (Hebrews 10:36, ESV).

In other words, we don't ever give up. We don't quit. Because we are not of those who shrink back. We keep searching even when treasures are hard to find. We keep helping even when the situation seems hopeless. And we keep believing even when the mission seems impossible. So my friend, let those eight words fill your tank and provide fuel for your journey. I'm just one of the many voices you'll hear cheering you on.

Don't wait until you feel confident to exercise courage. God's Word reminds us that we are given all we need for life and godliness.[11] You too are cheery, bold, and colorful, so live like it! As you do, you will find that a small risk is far more exciting than a big rut.

"Have I not commanded you? Be strong and courageous! Do not tremble or be dismayed, for the LORD your God is with you wherever you go" (Joshua 1:9, NASB).

If you see a forty-something lady walking down the street with leather pants, a pink suede jacket, and a white cane, just chalk her up to the ranks of those who can't quite manage confidence...but have enough courage in Jesus to make up for it.

CHAPTER FIVE

——— ✦ ———

Carry No Baggage

I was given a lovely bracelet at a recent speaking event in Lawrenceville, Georgia. In fact, all five hundred women attending the ladies' night out received the very same bracelet.

Just above the knives at each woman's place setting lay a stretchy, shiny, silver charm bracelet. They're the kind I call "happy bracelets." You know what I mean. They clink and clatter and jingle when they are jostled. They sound happy just to be on your wrist.

The bracelet was strung with charms resembling women's shoes—stylish stilettos. I loved it, especially since my wrist was the only place my body would ever safely wear such fashionable footwear.

The bracelet was a creative way for the host church to communicate the evening's theme: *walking by faith*.

I thought it was a fabulous idea.

But there was one problem.

Between each shoe on the bracelet hung a woman's purse. Yes, it was cute, but what do purses have to do with walking by faith? To my linear way of thinking, it diluted the whole theme of the evening. The cute purses, trendy and tiny as they were, detracted from the message of the bracelet.

Then, as I slipped it on my wrist, it hit me.

Purses have everything to do with walking by faith. The shoes are an obvious reminder to do as Paul tells us in 2 Corinthians 5:7—to walk by faith, not by sight. And the purses are an equally important reminder to carry no baggage.

BAGGAGE CLAIMS US

The person who thrives in a dark world and perseveres cannot be encumbered by the heavy things of life. Most of the things that weigh us down are the things we pick up along the way. This kind of baggage might seem attractive at the time— unforgiveness that seems justified, selfishness that seems harmless, prayerlessness that seems warranted, envy that we keep to ourselves.

Most of the baggage we gather is grabbed on impulse. We think we can afford it. It doesn't seem expensive until we realize we never quit paying for it. We convince ourselves we can own and manage it, until it dawns on us that our luggage owns *us* and we are managed by it.

So here's my confession: I've had to clean out my spiritual closet once or twice a season because I collect so much baggage. Are you a baggage collector like me?

A friend of mine who hadn't traveled much told me about finding himself weighted down on a rare business trip. He had been sick a few days before the trip and felt weak anyway; he also had a garment bag over one shoulder, a laptop computer in its case strapped over the other, a bag in one hand, and a briefcase in the other. (Clearly, no one had ever shown this guy how to pack.)

He was waiting for the bus at an airport kiosk to transport him to the rental car facility. When the bus rolled up, the doors opened and—he couldn't move. While the bus driver and people standing behind him waited, he found himself without the strength to lift his foot to the first step. His mind said "move," but his body just wouldn't.

That's what it's like when you're trying to move through life with heavy, bulky baggage biting into your shoulders and cramping your hands.

Thankfully, God has made a simple way to purge our lives of the harmful totes and heavy carry-ons we have collected. In the New Testament, the wise old apostle John tells us that if we confess our baggage, God is faithful and just to forgive us our baggage (see 1 John 1:9).

Actually, the Bible uses the word *sin*. But really, isn't that what baggage is? Don't let what seems like cute, trendy baggage keep you from walking well. It will weigh you down, immobilize you, and cause you to stumble.

You can't carry as much as you think. Things like unforgiveness, selfishness, and prayerlessness are really very heavy bags to haul. Sometimes we have no idea of how heavy that heaped-up load has become until we finally release it...and feel that wonderful sense of lightness, rest, and relief.

Sinful baggage manifests its ugly self in all sorts of ways. No matter what form it takes, however, it always bears one completely predictable element: It is rooted in self, not God. Ouch. I know that is not pleasant to hear, but deep down, you know it's true. At the center of any sin, all sin, is the letter "I." *Me, my way, mine.* No matter how you spell it, it all sounds the same. The letter "I" will always be at the center of sin.

THE KING—AND "I"

As pagan kings go, Nebuchadnezzar is definitely one of my favorites. At least, he's one of the most intriguing. Nebuchadnezzar was the notorious ruler of the great Babylonian Empire, and he began his reign four hundred years before the King of kings stepped onto our planet. He ruled over the world capital of Babylon for forty-three amazing years, and during his tenure he beautified and fortified his great city. Temples, waterways, and the wondrous hanging gardens— one of the seven wonders of the ancient world—were all of his royal doing. The historian Herodotus claimed that the outer walls of the city were 56 miles in length, 80 feet thick, and 320 feet high.

King Nebuchadnezzar, the greatest and most powerful of

all Babylonian kings, was a proud and boastful man. You might remember him from the Old Testament book of Daniel, when he was so impressed with himself that he erected a magnificent, ninety-foot-tall image of gold—almost three times higher than your average telephone pole—in his own honor. It was kind of like a fourth-century-B.C. Trump Towers. This king had absolutely no self-esteem issues. *Me, mine, my,* and *I* were undoubtedly his most frequently used words.

And then one night he had a very troubling dream. Something told him this was more than the cold pizza he'd eaten before bedtime. The dream came from God Himself.

After consulting all his counselors and advisors, Nebuchadnezzar remembered Daniel the Hebrew, a man on his staff who was known to walk with God.

Daniel interpreted the dream and didn't mince words with his boss. Unless something changed in the king's life, unless he got rid of his heavy baggage of sin, it was going to drag him down. *Way* down.

Here's what Daniel said: "So, king, take my advice: Make a clean break with your sins and start living for others. Quit your wicked life and look after the needs of the down-and-out. Then you will continue to have a good life" (Daniel 4:27, *The Message*).

It was good, hard-hitting counsel—and certainly not the kind of flattery he was used to. And maybe he thought about it for a while. But eventually he shrugged it off and became enamored again with his own pride and power.

That all changed, however, one fateful day. His pride

finally caused him to cross the line and fall under God's judgment.

Where was the line? What was the last piece of luggage that finally pulled him off his feet? Only God knew. And one fine day as the king was strolling on the high balcony of his royal palace, looking out over the marvelous city, he said to himself, "Look at this, Babylon the great! And I built it all by myself, a royal palace adequate to display my honor and glory!" (Daniel 4:30, *The Message*).

Just that quickly, in a moment of swelling pride, Nebuchadnezzar lost it. In an instant. The lights were on but no one was home. He went crazy. The ancient Greeks called this kind of madness *lycanthropy*. The victim imagines himself a beast. He leaves all human activity and takes on the lifestyle and demeanor of an animal.

For seven unbelievable years, Nebuchadnezzar was struck with this strange malady. From a palace to a pasture, the confused king made his abode among the cows and donkeys, "eating grass like an ox."

The king's pride weighed more than he knew, and that was some pretty costly luggage to carry. The baggage weighed him down—way, way down. It pulled him off his throne, out of his palace, out of the city, and literally down on his hands and knees like a four-footed beast.

His sin cost him far more than he ever thought he would have to pay. That's what pride does.

Pride makes the spotlight on me, myself, and I shine so brightly that everything and everyone else falls into the shadows.

If, before his fall, the king had been speaking in today's vernacular, he would have said: "My way, my looks, my brains, my rule, my skill, my clout, my stuff."

Do you ever sound like that? I will be the first to admit that this self-appointed monarch sits on her throne and spouts the same from time to time. We all struggle with sin. It's ugly and it's dangerous. Just look what it did to this high-and-mighty world ruler.

Baggage is heavy to carry, costly to store, and expensive to own. Maybe it's time to clean out the closet?

GETTING RID OF THE UNMENTIONABLES

For about ten years now, Katharyn, Lori, and I have met for a girls' weekend. Beach condos, New York City hotels, and even our homes have all played host to our once-a-year estrogen-charged escapes.

This year, we chose Kansas City for our latest installment. We arrived late Thursday night to discover that our lovely suite overlooked the Country Club Plaza. My expectations and excitement were brimming. The only thing I anticipated more than the shopping was the emptying of my brimming bladder. It had been a *long* drive.

After checking in, I raced into our hotel bathroom and quickly shut the door. Well, I tried to shut the door. Something had lodged beneath it and the door was jammed. I reached down to dislodge the assumed washcloth, grasped a wad of fabric in my fist—and screamed.

Katharyn and Lori rushed to the scene for a "sight" inspection. I knew for certain when Katharyn yelled, "Gross!" and Lori groaned.

I held an anonymous pair of men's underwear in my hand.

We all marched from the restroom to the phone. I pressed zero and connected with the young man at the front desk.

"How may I help you?" he said in a smooth, professional voice.

"There's *men's underwear* in my bathroom!" I exploded.

"I'm sorry, ma'am." (What else could he say?)

I stumbled and stuttered until he interrupted with "I'll send someone up." And so we stood near the door as far from the offending garment as possible, and waited for the attendant.

Five minutes...ten minutes...twenty minutes passed— and no one came to our rescue.

I could no longer restrain my righteous indignation. This was not right. Girls' weekend had been violated. The "strictly forbidden" list included testosterone, remote controls, football, and yes, men's underwear.

As Katharyn and Lori sat by the door, I quickened my pace back to the bathroom, picked up my cane, and stabbed those "whitey tighties" with the tip of my walking stick.

Like a spear gun in the belly of its prey, I proved to that mass of cotton who was boss. I marched toward the door, with cane pointed toward the heavens, and commanded, "Katharyn, open the door!" She did, and out flew the skivvies into the hallway. We roared with laughter as I again picked up the phone and informed the delinquent desk clerk that the underwear were now in the hallway.

Katharyn watched through the peephole, and sure enough, hotel personnel arrived in five minutes to disinfect the hallway.

So what's the point of this story? That there are some things in our lives that simply don't belong. Men's Fruit of the Loom underwear do not belong in a girls' bathroom on girls' weekend. It would be out of place, out of order, out of bounds, out of sync, and out of the question for us to leave them lying around. I guess that's pretty obvious. But it should be just as obvious that a child of the King would never tolerate such unmentionables as pride, envy, gossip, hidden malice, or any other such baggage lying around in her personal life.

It doesn't fit. It doesn't belong. It's an offense.

These things get in the way of what God has planned for you. Instead of enjoying the pleasure of the palace as God intended, the baggage of sin weighs you down and you end up in a pasture—becoming something and someone you were never intended to be.

That's when it's time for real righteous indignation.

Don't hover and huddle by the door, waiting for sin to march itself out of your life. Instead, stride forward by faith. Stare it down, use the tools God gave you to conquer it, and then fling it out of your life. You might need someone to open the door for you, or walk beside you, but don't let precious plans and your purposeful life be derailed by something that doesn't belong there.

TOOLS FOR BAGGAGE REMOVAL

Now, my friend, you really ought to listen to me because I have more experience with sin removal than I would like to admit.

I have found two particular tools from God's Word especially helpful. So just in case you've got some excess baggage—or perhaps discovered a few unmentionables that need to be "flung"—let me open the door and guide you through it.

The first tool in the box might be a surprise. It's the law. Yikes! Don't be nervous. The law wasn't given for your condemnation; it was given to lead you to real life.

The law makes us "conscious of sin" (Romans 3:20). Without the law we'd never know the standard, the rules. Life would be a game in which we haphazardly move the pieces without knowing how to reach the real destination. God's law lays a foundation for life by making us aware of the sin that keeps us separated from our Father and Creator.

The law also makes us accountable for our sin (Romans 5:13). Now, you might not believe me at first, but this truth really should lighten your load. Sin separates us from God, and if God did not hold us accountable for our sin, we'd never be able to find an approach to Him at all. Knowing the truth about our sin paves the pathway to His presence. And remember what Jesus told us about the truth: It sets us free (John 8:32). (I feel a little lighter already.)

Lastly, the law leads us to Christ (Galatians 3:24). Jesus is the real destination of life. He is the pinnacle at the end of the pathway. He is our pursuit, our longing, the desire of nations. All we could ever want or need, we find in Him. But without the law, we'd never know the way. The law is the tool that leads to life and clarity because it shines the spotlight on our unmentionables. It makes us aware of our sin, exposes our need, and leads us to grace. The law is like a road map that leads to the cross. And that's the only place you can leave your baggage.

The second tool in the box is repentance. This is what God empowers us to do. *We don't have to carry those heavy bags around from place to place.* He has provided a way for us to drop that ugly luggage, turn from sin, and fling it out of our lives. The Greek word for repentance is *metanoeo*. It means to change one's mind, one's direction. In what direction are you walking?

Proverbs 28:13 says, "He who conceals his sins does not prosper, but whoever confesses and renounces them finds mercy." First John 1:9 reminds us that our God is faithful. If you do confess your sins, He will forgive you. He will cleanse you from all the unrighteousness your baggage represents.

It simply takes agreement with God.

What He calls dirt, you call dirt.

What He labels excess baggage, you label the same way.

What He names as an offending garment that has no place in your life, you agree and pitch it out.

It's an about-face, a 180. Nebuchadnezzar came to that place after seven long, humbling years, and both his kingdom and his sanity were restored (Daniel 4:34).

Do you need to change your mind? Do you need to turn around and walk in the other direction? Do you need to wield this tool of repentance? In order to finish well, in order to run with endurance, you must be heading in the right direction—and carrying no baggage.

God's Word is the light that guides us; it's the laser beam that focuses on our need, the warm glow that beckons us to come. The tool of the law guides us to repentance. The tool of repentance grants us restored relationship with God through the grace of Jesus Christ. It is God's amazing grace that leads us through the twists and turns of this life.

Ultimately, it is the grace of God that takes us from darkness to light. In the words of John Newton, "'Tis grace that brought me safe thus far, and grace will lead me home."

You don't need any baggage for that trip Home, however long it may be. God Himself will provide you with everything you need.

Travel light, my friend.

CHAPTER SIX

Obey the Grace Rules

"Miss, where is she seated?"

When the gentleman seated in first class spoke up, the flight attendant who was guiding me down the cramped aisle of the 737 paused.

Where was *I* seated? I immediately quipped, "Not up here!"

The flight attendant replied that my seat was near the back of the plane. Hearing that, the businessman grabbed his carry-on bag and excused himself over the other passenger in his row. "I'll take her seat," he told the attendant. "She can have mine."

"Are you sure?" I asked. I could hardly believe my ears.

After all, he had paid good money for a first-class ticket. He had the opportunity to enjoy china dishes, cloth napkins, hovering flight attendants, and pampering. I was destined for peanuts, leg cramps, and a can of lukewarm Coke.

He patted my shoulder as he walked back toward my seat. "I want to," he assured me.

I was humbled. "Thank you," I said, sinking into the wide leather seat—the very lap of airline luxury.

What a great surprise! What grace.

GRACE RULES

According to the rules, my coach-class ticket bound me to coach seating. But grace has its own set of rules. And when the grace rules overrule the regular rules...well, that's what we call unmerited benevolence, undeserved favor.

Grace has nothing to do with fairness or equity. Grace gives to the undeserving, forgives the guilty, and covers the unworthy. Grace sits in the back of the plane so you can have the front seat.

The law, on the other hand, judges strictly, shows no mercy, demands compliance, and exposes guilt (Romans 8:2). Which set of rules would you rather be under?

The sons of Aaron the priest were under the rule of law rather than the rule of grace. Because of His white-hot holiness, God instituted a protocol—strict step-by-step procedures—by which man should approach Him.[12] But one day Aaron's sons chose to freelance a little, presumptuously stepping outside the protection provided by God's set of rules.

Now Nadab and Abihu, the sons of Aaron, took their respective fire pans, and after putting fire in them, placed incense on it and offered strange fire before the LORD, which He had not commanded them. And fire came out from the presence of the LORD and consumed them, and they died before the LORD. (Leviticus 10:1–2, NASB)

Aaron's sons showed up in the presence of the Lord with their own manufactured worship, not as the Lord had required. It wasn't that God was angry or out to make a point. As twentieth-century evangelist Vance Havner put it, "We do not really break the laws of God, we break ourselves against them. We do not break the law of gravitation by jumping from a skyscraper, we break our necks."

In other words, Nadab and Abihu simply fell under the law of the holiness of God—something that cannot be trifled with or taken lightly.

Aaron's sons aren't the only people mentioned in the Bible who suffered the consequences of the law when they tried to pave their own roads to God. God rejected Cain's sacrifice of fruits and vegetables because it did not meet His requirements.[13] Uzzah helped carry the ark of God back to Jerusalem. But when he touched the ark, he was immediately struck dead. Why? Because the law forbade anyone to touch the ark of the covenant, which represented the presence of God among His people.[14]

Aaron's sons, Cain, and Uzzah all learned the harsh reality of the law when they violated its unbending rules:

Sinful man simply cannot stand before holy God on his own terms and live.[15] Period. End of discussion.

When I consider truths like these, I sometimes wonder why I'm still around—why I haven't been fried on the spot like Nadab and Abihu. Why aren't we consumed or rejected when we clumsily approach Him? Why aren't we instantly vaporized when our sinfulness collides with His holiness? Why aren't we subject to the same law as Aaron's sons? After all, He is the same God. And we are much like the sons of Aaron. We offer to God our own versions of *strange fire*. We show up in the presence of the Lord with hypocrisy or indifference, pride or disregard. Simply put...sin. Sin that cannot stand safely before the holiness of God. God will always exercise justice concerning sin. He has to. His holiness will permit no less.

So how can we stand before God? One of the most poignant lessons I have ever learned in the Light is...grace. Jesus absorbed the penalty for sin that should have been directed toward us.[16] That is the very heart of the issue. That is the essence of grace.

Because of His death, we live.[17]

Because He became poor, we are now rich.[18]

God gives His grace so we can meet His demand of holiness—and live. And serve Him and walk with Him and approach Him and enjoy Him.

GRACE IN A GOURD

There once was a well-known prophet who might have taken a refresher course on the grace rules. His graceless prejudice led him down the path of a prodigal. God called Jonah to be His man, His prophet, and chose to sign him up for a much needed lesson on the rules of grace.

God told Jonah to alert the people living in the Assyrian capital of Nineveh to the imminent destruction of their city. But Jonah hated the Assyrians for their arrogance and cruelty and atrocities against his people; instead of heeding the Lord's call, he sprinted away from God and Nineveh and fell fast asleep in the belly of a storm tossed ship. Then he stepped forward to be thrown overboard, exchanging a ship's belly for a fish's belly. (That's the CliffNotes version of the story. You'll find all the details in the Old Testament book of Jonah.)

Jonah's journey from a fishy fortress to a hillside hideout tells us a lot about the meaning of grace. In the well-worn story of Jonah's deliverance from the fish, God puts His undeserved kindness on display by saving Jonah's life and renewing his calling, even though Jonah was unworthy.

After reluctantly carrying out his duty, Jonah set up camp on a knoll overlooking the city he despised. There he waited—sulking and yearning for God to annihilate the people who had just turned *en masse* to the God of Israel. Then he had the audacity to whimper and whine and rant and rave at God, who had hurled him to and fro through the digestive juices of an anonymous but very great fish.

Jonah wanted the Ninevites to feast on a banquet of just deserts. He savored the idea of God's justice raining down fire and brimstone upon the people. I imagine him sitting back with a bowl of popcorn and waiting for the fireworks to begin as God gave the people of Nineveh what they deserved.

Funny, isn't it? Jonah didn't get what he deserved...but he certainly wanted the Ninevites to. Only trouble was, the fireworks display got called off. The brimstone never fell. The disaster passed them by. Deep down, Jonah knew it would turn out that way. And it made him boil over with anger.

Thoroughly disgusted, he told the Lord, "I knew that you are a gracious and compassionate God, slow to anger and abounding in love, a God who relents from sending calamity" (Jonah 4:2).

God demands justice because He is judge, but He offers grace because He is good. When it came to the Assyrians, Jonah wanted God to be one-dimensional. He wanted harsh justice and vengeance. Earlier in the book, Jonah had claimed God's grace. But there was no way he wanted to share that grace with Nineveh. Jonah, who had received grace, was unwilling to grant it.

If I were God, I think at this point I would have lost it with that prejudiced, ungrateful prophet—maybe turning him back into fish bait. Wouldn't you? That's just like me to think in those terms—but it's not how God responded. Rather than returning Jonah to his sunken sanctuary or pitching out a few well-placed lightning bolts to teach him a lesson, God cultivated a living parable to instruct Jonah in the profound schoolroom of grace.

The LORD God provided a vine and made it grow up over Jonah to give shade for his head to ease his discomfort, and Jonah was very happy about the vine. (Jonah 4:6)

Jonah once again received grace. Grace in a vine, which the King James Version describes as a "gourd." The prophet was glad for the vine, but he was not grateful. He took comfort in its shade when he could have found ultimate satisfaction in the shadow of God's wings.

The prophet, who had over and over been the recipient of God's amazing grace, became the judge. And the almighty Judge became the patron of grace.

Sadly enough, I can relate to Jonah. I understand his perspective far better than I can comprehend God's incomprehensible grace. However, I also agree with something Vance Havner once said: "I do not understand all about electricity, but I don't intend to sit in the dark until I do." That's how I feel about grace. Grace calls prodigals to be prophets and turns pagans into parishioners.

One thing is for certain: If not for grace, our world would be dark, merciless, and...exactly what we deserve. As Scripture says, we would be without hope and without God in the world.[19] The hymn writers have fittingly called grace amazing, wonderful, marvelous, matchless, and greater than all my sin. Grace is all those things and more.

But it is never fair.

THAT'S NOT FAIR!

Grace by its very nature is unfair. We don't "deserve" such bountiful excess—not even close.

The apostle Paul understood very well the staggering unfairness of this grace. He also knew it was sufficient to meet his every need, though it took a thorn for Paul to learn that lesson. Paul asked God, in 2 Corinthians 12:8, to remove the painful thorn in his flesh. He evidently struggled with some difficult circumstance that he really wanted changed.

His thorn could have been anything; physical, emotional, spiritual. The Bible doesn't clarify exactly what his thorn was. Why not? Maybe so that we could all better identify with the results of that affliction—pain, discomfort, and a longing for it to be removed.

We all have thorns. For me, blindness is a neverending, constantly challenging, fatigue inducing thorn. I can't deny it: It hurts. I've often longed for it to go away.

What is your thorn? What makes you, like Paul, beg God for a little divine surgery?

I wonder whether Paul considered his thorn unfair. We do know that Paul asked God to remove it and God responded. God, who is always fair and is well qualified and quite capable of "thorn removal," answered with something even better than immediate release or deliverance. That something was His grace.[20]

We can all imagine how Paul must have felt. We tell ourselves, *If only my thorn would be miraculously, instantaneously removed, that would be enough for me.*

But as much as we would like to convince God that thorn removal would be sufficient, God knows best that only one thing is sufficient: His grace.

Trust me, my friend, the longer I live in physical darkness yet in the light of His Word, the more convinced I become that healing is not sufficient.

Deliverance is not sufficient.

Restored relationships are not sufficient.

Finding a life partner is not sufficient.

Material provision is not sufficient.

Fame and popularity are not sufficient.

Perfect health and a sculpted body are not sufficient.

Each of these things is a joyous blessing in itself, but they are not enough. *Never* enough.

If healing or "thorn removal" in and of itself were sufficient for the apostle Paul, then surely heaven would have granted it.

But God had something wider, higher, deeper, broader, more miraculous and enduring in mind. Paul wouldn't get what he asked for because he didn't understand what he needed more than anything else. If he had simply and instantly been healed of his malady (whatever it was), he would have missed something far greater than he could have conceived.

Healing can't be compared to the grace of God, alive and at work in our lives. Comfort and stress relief and health and paid bills can't even be recorded on the same ledger with the power of God surging through our brokenness, want, and need, and becoming perfect in our weakness.

The grace of Jesus Christ is better than anything. God's lovingkindness is better than life itself. Don't settle for a merely adequate and temporary answer to your prayer, when God may be granting you the lasting and deeper gift of grace.

And sometimes, perhaps even most times, that grace is best realized in our thorns.

Grace will not take you away from the pains and disappointments and limitations and heartaches of life on a broken planet. But it will sustain you, deepen you, strengthen you, change you, and overflow your life in a way that simple deliverance from pain or hardship never could.

Grace is enough. It is enough to sustain you when the thorns hurt, enough to cover you when you bow before Him in your sinfulness. The psalmist said:

> If you, O LORD, should mark iniquities,
> O Lord, who could stand?
> But with you there is forgiveness,
> that you may be feared.
> (Psalm 130:3–4, ESV)

God's grace truly is amazing, unfair, and sufficient. The reason God's grace is sufficient is because it is both priceless and practical.

Priceless

When my friend Karen returned from England, she told me about visiting the Tower of London and beholding the stunning crown jewels of Great Britain.

"I asked an attentive and well-accented Beefeater about the value of the crown jewels," she told me, "and instead of an answer, I received an education."

The guard explained to Karen that the jewels lend their splendor to coronations and jubilees as symbols of royalty, authority, justice, and spirituality. They remain a tangible link, he said, between modern-day England and the kings and queens of long ago. He told Karen that the jewels have been housed in the Tower for nearly a millennium and pointed with pride to the 530.2-carat Great Star of Africa, the world's second largest cut diamond.

The Beefeater's final bit of information, however, came as a shock to Karen: As to stated value, the storied jewels have none. That's hard to believe until you ask, How could you put a price on such magnificence? The jewels possess far more than a superlative intrinsic value. Their symbolism, history, and tradition cannot be appraised. They are irreplaceable and without comparison; no price tag could do them justice.

So it is with grace, though perhaps we don't have eyes to see it or hearts that truly understand it. Grace has no equal, and its value goes far beyond imagery, history, and tradition. Grace was "...bought with a price" (1 Corinthians 7:23, NASB). Philip Yancey wrote that grace "contains the essence of the gospel as a drop of water can contain the image of the sun."

What does grace cost? Well, it cost Jesus His very lifeblood.

For you know that it was not with perishable things such as silver or gold that you were redeemed from the empty way of life handed down to you from your forefathers, but with the precious blood of Christ, a lamb without blemish or defect. (1 Peter 1:18–19)

If the worth of the crown jewels—basically a pile of shiny rocks, when you think about it—cannot be measured, then what of the blood of God's own Son? It is a question that confounds even the angels.[21]

Grace Shows Up

Karen's husband, Gerry, showed the practical side of grace while shopping with his kids at Target recently.

As Gerry made his way through the aisles picking up a few essentials, he tried to demonstrate the concept of grace to his two children. He told them that grace is God's "unmerited favor." When that phrase generated a blank stare, he explained that it's getting something we don't deserve and haven't earned.

He illustrated his point by taking a detour from the usual aisles lined with laundry detergent and paper towels and heading straight for the toy department. His wide-eyed children quickly decided that if grace had something to do with toys, it must be worth learning about.

He knelt beside his little ones and told them they could choose any toy they wanted—up to ten dollars. (Daddy's grace may be without limit, but his checkbook isn't.) Neither Maddie nor Mason asked any questions. They searched the toy-strewn lanes for just the right prized possessions, and then gleefully watched as their daddy paid the bill and handed over the goods—which they received with joy.

Gerry tells me that he knows his kids got the message because now whenever they see a Target sign, Mason asks, "Daddy, can we have a little grace?"

In the Bible, the Hebrew word for *gracious* is used almost

exclusively of God.[22] It denotes the action which springs from His free, unmerited kindness toward us. God's ultimate expression of grace was in Christ, through whom grace and truth came to us.[23]

Grace is no abstract quality or starry-eyed lover dreaming fanciful dreams. It is an active, personal principle showing itself in the way we deal with others and in the way God deals with us.

In other words, grace shows up.

Grace shows up when "[God] causes his sun to rise on the evil and the good, and sends rain on the righteous and the unrighteous" (Matthew 5:45). Grace arrives to show us that He "does not treat us as our sins deserve or repay us according to our iniquities" (Psalm 103:10).

Grace showed up when Jesus restored a demon possessed man.[24] Grace revealed Jesus as Messiah to a Samaritan woman.[25] Grace gave dignity to another woman shamed by adultery.[26] Grace reinstated Peter, who had openly denied Christ.[27] And Grace called Saul, the persecutor of saints, to become Paul, the preacher of the gospel.[28]

Grace is priceless and practical. And it's also paid for. When we sing "Jesus paid it all," we're really saying that grace covers our debts, credits our account, finances our investments, yields a capital reserve in the depository of eternity, and then bestows "an inheritance that can never perish, spoil or fade—kept in heaven for you" (1 Peter 1:4).

Before I lost my sight, I remember curiously staring at those 3-D stereogram pictures. They look like a bunch of random nonsense until you stare at them long enough to see the real image pop right out at you. Then, once you see the image, you can't *not* see it.

Grace is like that. It might not seem to make any sense at first, and it might take some time and focus to perceive it correctly. But once you do, there's no going back.

Grace is the great surprise of salvation. It's an unexpected trip to the toy department, an undeserved seat in first class. Where the law demands, grace delivers. When the law hands down a verdict, grace sets us free. It is a gift, not a payment. It is benevolence, not reimbursement. It is kindness, compassion, generosity, and goodwill.

When situations fail us, when the familiar ground crumbles away beneath our very feet, grace mounts us on eagle's wings. When daily issues confront our sensibilities, grace carries us to the heights. When disappointment, suffering, or thorns hurt us, grace is the gentle covering that blankets our lives with everlasting incorruptibility.

Grace doesn't fluctuate with the stock market or fly away when the winds blow hard. It doesn't fade, diminish, or hesitate. Grace stands the test of time.

It is unmerited favor.

It is undeserved kindness.

It is sufficient, unearned, priceless, practical, and unreasonable.

And yes, completely, blessedly, eternally unfair.

The LORD longs to be gracious to you; he rises to show you compassion. For the LORD is a God of justice. Blessed are all who wait for him! (Isaiah 30:18)

CHAPTER SEVEN

Become Meek and Mighty

After my new guide dog, William, and I had been home together for a few weeks, I realized we had a big problem. William—my bouncy, eager, loyal yellow Labrador—could not get over his food obsession.

When we were in training at the "dog school," William and I went through rigorous behavior-modifying techniques to help break him of his food focus. But even after several daily doughnut walks (you'll have to read *Lessons I Learned in the Dark* for the doughnut drama), William still had an appetite for the forbidden.

So I left the dog school with specific training instructions to help William with his food issues. Since there were no canine support groups where dogs stood on all fours and confessed,

"My name is William, and I am a foodaholic," the burden for his recovery rested on my shoulders. That meant each morning, when he was good and hungry, I would set William's food before him. But then I would instruct him to *stay*.

The trainers at the school told me to continue this until my dog showed a degree of self-control. Ah, poor William. He would sit six inches away from his brimming bowl, his nose extended as far as possible, his neck completely contorted. He would quiver all over and whine piteously until I gave him the "go" sign.

Every day William and I performed this difficult task, and every day it got a little better than the day before. Each day he would whine less, quiver less, and control himself more. One day I began the usual routine, called William, told him to sit and stay, poured his food, and left the kitchen.

I waited around the corner and listened. No chomping. No whining.

Good, I said to myself. *He's recovered from his addiction.*

Just as I was rounding the corner to give him the "go" sign, the phone rang. I picked it up and became engrossed in a long, soap opera–style conversation. After I hung up, I realized how late it was getting and quickly made my way into my room to get dressed for the day.

When I was all dressed, I walked back into the kitchen for a glass of water. And there sat William. Alert. Hopeful. Obedient. Forgotten. I had left him there in front of his food for almost an hour. Of course I gave him the go-ahead and praised him profusely. I think I even gave him seconds that morning. William, even without his harness, acted with a bridled will, obedient and under control.

William was meek.

Not weak, but meek.

Someone has said, "Meekness does not identify the weak but more precisely the strong who have been placed in a position of weakness where they persevere without giving up." In other words, a meek person bears and wears his or her yoke.

A WELL-FITTED YOKE

There once was a humble carpenter who lived in ancient Palestine. He enjoyed the reputation of making the best yokes in all of Galilee. As a skilled craftsman, he would measure an ox, and then fashion a customized yoke for the animal from a piece of wood. Once the yoke was completed, the ox would be summoned to try on the masterpiece. If adjustments were needed, the carpenter would work a little more to make sure it fit just right.

People from all of Palestine came for his yokes. The carpenter worked daily in his little shop and used only the finest materials. From dawn to dusk he sculpted yokes of unparalleled craftsmanship. Farmers came from miles away for this gentle carpenter's handiwork, because none fit better. Anyone who came to Nazareth needing a well-fitting yoke could find his shop, because above the door hung a sign that read "My Yokes Fit Well."

I know about the little carpentry shop in Nazareth,

because I know the Carpenter. I happen to wear one of His yokes, and it does fit perfectly. In fact, His yoke is easy.

The yoke Jesus offers each of us is easy. Well fitting. I would walk millions of miles just to have the privilege of bearing it. You see, to be beneath the yoke of Christ is to enjoy a meek, submitted life.

When the ancient Jews spoke of "the yoke," they referred to one placing himself under submission. They were accustomed to submitting to the yoke of the law, the yoke of the kingdom, the yoke of the commandments, and the yoke of God. And to be honest, the yokes of which they spoke burdened and constrained them, and were a frequent source of discouragement.

That's why the words of Jesus the Carpenter must have felt as free and refreshing as a summer breeze: "Take My yoke upon you and learn from Me," He said, "for I am gentle and lowly in heart, and you will find rest for your souls. For My yoke is easy and My burden is light" (Matthew 11:29–32, NKJV).

Can you imagine what His Jewish audience must have thought as they listened to such inviting words? Can you imagine how they must have felt? When you personalize His words, you will find that His yoke is an invitation to enjoy a meek will.

When Jesus used the word *easy* to describe His yoke, the Jewish listeners heard something very different from what you and I might perceive today. When we hear the word *easy*, we might think of "simple" or "uncomplicated." But the Greek word for *easy* in this verse can mean "well fitting." His yoke is crafted, not by an earthly carpenter's hands, but from your heavenly Carpenter's heart. It fits perfectly, because He knows how a yoke feels. He wears the yoke of His Father.

MODEL OF MEEKNESS

As Jesus passed through Capernaum, a Roman centurion flagged him down. I can just see the powerful official gasp, trying to catch his breath as he ran to tell Jesus, "Lord, my servant is lying at home paralyzed, dreadfully tormented" (Matthew 8:6, NKJV).

Jesus must have gazed with great intention into the eyes of the concerned yet confident centurion when He graciously offered to go to the officer's home and heal his beloved servant.

> The centurion answered and said, "Lord, I am not worthy that You should come under my roof. But only speak a word, and my servant will be healed. For I *also* am a man under authority, having soldiers under me. And I say to this one, 'Go,' and he goes; and to another, 'Come,' and he comes; and to my servant, 'Do this,' and he does it." (Matthew 8:8–9, NKJV, emphasis mine)

The centurion's big faith usually takes center stage in this story, but I want to shine the spotlight on one little word: *also.* You read it in verse 9. The centurion acknowledged that just like himself, Jesus was a man of authority and also a man under authority. The centurion knew he possessed power because he had submitted himself to the powerful Roman authority.

The centurion recognized that Christ possessed authority because He bore the yoke of His Father. His authority was supreme, because He was submitted to ultimate authority.

Jesus had been telling His disciples as much while they traveled the dusty miles together.

"For I did not speak on My own initiative, but the Father Himself who sent Me has given Me a commandment as to what to say and what to speak.... Do you not believe that I am in the Father, and the Father is in Me? The words that I say to you I do not speak on My own initiative, but the Father abiding in Me does His works.... So that the world may know that I love the Father, I do exactly as the Father commanded Me." (John 12:49; 14:10, 31, NASB)

The centurion acknowledged both Jesus' inherent authority and His submission to authority. That's the most remarkable part of this story as far as I'm concerned, because this Gentile man had clued in to what few others had even noticed. Jesus possessed all power and authority but at the same time, submitted Himself to the power and authority of Another.

Beautiful, isn't it? Jesus is the ultimate picture of meekness.

To be meek is to recognize our own personal power and willingly submit it to the authority of another. That's what our Savior did. And in His meekness was majesty.

In the Sermon on the Mount, Jesus made a radical proclamation concerning the meek. "Blessed are the meek, for they will inherit the earth" (Matthew 5:5). Only meekness can make that possible. To be meek is to have control over sin and self. If we were truly meek—our wills bridled to the extent that we had mastery over ourselves and our sin— how strong we would be. God would be free to bless us and use us to our full potential.

MEEKNESS HAS A BACKBONE

Rosa Parks was a God-fearing, churchgoing seamstress in Montgomery, Alabama. As she boarded the city bus one evening after work, she settled into a seat near the front. When a white man boarded, it was expected that she, a black woman, would willingly surrender her seat. After all, segregation on the public transit system in the South in 1955 was the law.

When Rosa quietly refused, she violated a city ordinance and, in her meekness, changed the course of American history. Certainly she had no idea that her gentle defiance on behalf of human dignity would spawn the civil rights movement.

That same night, forty black pastors came together and vowed to fight the segregation that plagued Montgomery's public transportation system. The Reverend Martin Luther King Jr. was chosen to lead the boycott. African Americans all over Montgomery walked and carpooled to work, enduring hatred and harassment.

One year later, the U.S. Supreme Court ruled that seg-regation violated the Constitution. History was forever altered, and it began with a quiet, gentle, meek refusal to obey that which was wrong, and a willingness to bravely take a risk for what was right.

Meekness is not simply doing what you are told. The person who is ordered to do something wrong or evil and automatically complies isn't meek. That's just cowardice.

True, God-ordained meekness can move mountains. Meekness was Jesus washing the feet of His disciples—and it was also Jesus clearing the temple with a whip. Meekness was Moses showing intolerance for his wayward people at the base of the mountain; meekness was a humble seam-stress refusing to give up her seat.

Meekness is not passive. It is active restraint, bridled control, and humbly motivated action. Meekness is the backbone of Christianity. It is a gift from the Holy Spirit (Galatians 5:22), yet it is up to us to unwrap it. Failure to receive the gift of meekness results in debilitating weakness.

WHEN WE AREN'T MEEK

Sometimes you hear that people who have been married a long time become so close they begin to take on one another's characteristics.

Well, maybe.

But I am rock-solid sure that there are some things about my husband and me that will never change. Phil, for instance, is a die-hard, card-carrying, fully committed, lifelong pack rat. And me? I tend toward the tightly wound, type A, *Good Housekeeping* Seal of approval—bearing neat freak.

As the years have gone by, however, I have become cheerfully resigned to our differences. Pack Rat and Neat Freak have made a go of it by learning to give and take—and with massive infusions of grace from the God who delights in marriages.

Late in the summer of 2003, however, in our seventeenth year of wedded bliss, we hit a speed bump. That's when I began nesting. I wasn't expecting a baby, but I was due to deliver a book manuscript to the publisher in a few months.

Knowing the months of labor that lay ahead, realizing what an all-consuming task waited just around the corner...I got the urge to purge. I simply felt like there was no way I could write my book if our storage room was in such a mess. (Only the type A reader will fully understand that statement.)

And so I attacked our basement storage room like a sugared-up, out-of-control child in a tae kwon do class. Don't stand in the way of a nesting woman with fire in her eyes. I marched in with steel determination and began kicking boxes outside and pitching old lampshades over my head and out the door. I really got into it. Let me just tell you, sufficient drive makes up for insufficient eyesight. I hung tools and filled boxes while my assistant filed papers from 1985.

In my frenzied cleaning, I ran my hand across the dusty speakers from an old sound system we had purchased when we were first married. I had traveled with that cumbersome system for five years, setting it up each time I sang. It hadn't seen the light of day for years.

The urge was strong upon me.

I *so* wanted to give it away.

I knew I had room in the truck. I knew Victory Mission would be blessed by such a generous donation. And I would be blessed to be rid of it.

And so, without consulting anybody and with no thought for Phil's opinion, I dragged three thousand dollars' worth of Yamaha, Peavey, and Bose equipment up the basement stairs and shoved them into the back of the truck.

After the delivery was made, I felt cleansed.

The cleaning compulsion had burned itself out for the time being, and now...I would be able to write that book. My muscles were sore but my head was clear, and my storage room was clean, clean, clean!

The next morning at 4:30, however, I awoke with an uncomfortable feeling. All I could think about was the sound system I had given away the day before. And then the questions came rolling along. *Why didn't you ask Phil before you gave the system away? Don't you think he'll notice it's gone? Whose sound system was it, anyway?*

I tried to mount a defense against the pangs besetting me. *I didn't ask him because he wouldn't have gotten rid of it. Anyway, did he ever sing over those microphones? No. It was my system...my decision.*

My defense wasn't cutting it. I was losing ground to a growing conviction. I tried to fall back asleep, but the thoughts kept hounding me. Finally rescued by my alarm clock, I jumped up and threw myself into the busy morning routine. But as soon as the last child left for school, the house became quiet...and my thoughts drew me back to some painful conclusions.

My actions had been unbridled. Out of control. I had wanted it my way and on my timetable. My mantra had been "I'd rather ask forgiveness than permission."

Oh, so clever. I hadn't been willing to consider anything or anyone outside of my will...not God, not Phil. And now, I was alone with my consequence. It wasn't the storage room that was dirty. It was my heart.

I went down to my writing room and knelt before the recliner where I often listen to God. I knew I had really blown it and needed to be cleansed. I asked God to forgive me for my intentional deceit and selfishness. He did...and then He prompted me to do what I dreaded most.

Call Phil at work.

Oh Lord, You know he'll never notice that it's missing. I threw stuff out of that room that he hasn't thought about in fifteen years!

But there was no getting around it. I knew I was to call, so I did. I told Phil what I had done and asked for his forgiveness. He was so disappointed, but even so he forgave me.

I hung up and decided that what I had wanted wasn't worth what I got. I wish I had stowed that bulky, outdated sound system in the back corner of my storage room so I could enjoy an uncluttered relationship with Phil. My former mantra was a lie. It's *not* easier to ask forgiveness than permission. No, not at all. You see, I love Phil and I love God's Word, and I violated both in a single act of willful volition.

Now I realize that it's good that the sound system is

gone. Not for the extra space in the storage room, but for what it exposed in my heart that desperately needed to go—an unbridled will.

Unbridled volition screams to the world, "It's my way or the highway," "I will because I can," and "I'd rather ask forgiveness than permission."

A surrendered will sings a different song. It isn't loud, it isn't shrill, it isn't flashy. But there's something about its understated melody that reaches into the deep places of the soul, satisfying at a whole different level. Meekness says, "I will seek permission so I won't have to seek forgiveness," and "Just because I can doesn't mean I should."

Unrestrained volition—a rampant, out of control will—invites wasted energy, frustration, and eventual self-destruction. However, meekness—a will bridled and cooperative—experiences a clean, uncluttered heart.

When I attempt to shrug off His perfect yoke, determining to go my own way and march under my own banner, I'm headed for a big fall. I will hurt myself, hurt others, and grieve the Lord's Spirit within me.

I'll be self-willed, and weak as a woman can be.

Our Lord's gracious invitation to submit to His well-fitted yoke still echoes through the ages, and resonates through the pages of Scripture. Strength is not the answer to power, control, or triumph. Meekness is. "It is not by strength that one prevails" (1 Samuel 2:9). When we unburden ourselves from the heavy weight of our own power, then we can bear the well-fitting yoke of Christ, and within His yoke, we learn meekness.

You can be strong willed and meek willed at the same time. A strong willed personality is a gift from God, and it serves those of us who have it very well. But it should never be an excuse for a lack of meekness.

Meekness marries the two virtues of strength and compliance.

And the benefits? Well, they simply never end. David tells us that God will personally guide the meek and teach them His way (Psalm 25:9). The Lord even told Isaiah that He values and *esteems* the man or woman who has learned the way of meekness (Isaiah 66:2).

Add to that, then, the promise of Jesus that the meek will inherit the world.

So why in the world do I expect to win by fighting for my own way? In fact, that is the surest path to defeat. And that's one of the best and hardest lessons I've learned in *the Light*.

CHAPTER EIGHT

Pray Like Crazy

Back in college, I remember being on a worship team with a friend named Paul. He was the most spiritually mature guy my age that I knew. Each week, our little team practiced our praise songs together so we'd be ready to lead the two hundred college students that gathered every Thursday night in the student center—Paul on the guitar and me on the piano.

I will never forget the time we had finished our rehearsal and began a time of prayer. This was our normal custom, to finish each session with prayer. But this time was different. The bass player and drummer had already left, and Paul and I were there alone.

Paul began to pray in a way I had never heard before. He

stretched himself across the floor, nose so close to the ground that I was sure he was inhaling carpet fiber. There I sat, head bowed, startled and still, sitting on the piano bench. How could I pray with this guy? He was obviously more connected with God than I was. After all, he had taken the "lying prostrate before the Lord" position.

In my mind, my posture of crossed legs and hands was not nearly as spiritual, and therefore not nearly as acceptable, to God. If my position wasn't sufficient, then there was no way that my words would have been.

Besides, who can pray when your mind is filled with comparison and self-analysis? I just listened to Paul, agreeing with his heartfelt words. When he finished, I muttered something like "Me too" or "I agree, Lord." I was a ball of mixed emotions and conflicting thoughts.

Prayer had left me feeling confused and silent instead of secure and conversational, as God intended. Was it Paul's fault? No way. It was all about my being more concerned with the method and mechanics of prayer than the motives and meaning.

The truth was, I was intimidated. Intimidated by prayer. I had become so preoccupied with my own perceived deficiencies that I lost the joy of simply coming into the presence of my heavenly Father who loved me.

Prayer *still* intimidates me at times.

There. I said it. That's my confession; do with it what you will. Hesitant as I may be to admit it, I have to own up to the truth. In fact, I've been known to work myself into a spiritual frenzy of hesitation and second-guessing before I say the first word to God. ...*How much prayer is enough? Are my motives pure? Are my petitions selfish or shallow? Will God be offended if my mind wanders?*

Do you ever ask yourself those kinds of questions? I suspect we all do. But the great lesson I've learned in the Light is profound and simple.

Are you ready?

Just pray.

Pray anyway. Pray constantly. Pray right through all those doubts and questions. Yes, intimidated or not, pray...pray like crazy. Vance Havner boiled it all down when he said: "If you can't pray like you want to, pray as you can. God knows what you mean."

OUR INTERPRETER

God knows how we struggle in prayer. Of course He does. He's never overlooked anything, ever, and He never will. The word *overlook* isn't even in His vocabulary.

He knows our situation... He knows that we are flawed, fallen-yet-redeemed human beings on a rebel planet that is temporarily under the control of the evil one.

He knows our weakness... David assures us that "He Himself knows our frame; He is mindful that we are but dust" (Psalm 103:14, NASB). God is totally aware of our physical, mental, and emotional struggles when we attempt to pray.

He knows our circumstances... There isn't a single event, concern, worry, or pressure in our lives that slips His notice. Job reminds us that "He knows the way I take" (Job 23:10, NASB).

Knowing all these things, understanding that you and I will sometimes find prayer difficult or discouraging, God gave us some powerful help. Paul writes, "The Spirit helps us in our weakness; for we do not know how to pray as we ought, but the Spirit himself intercedes for us with sighs too deep for words. And he who searches the hearts of men knows what is the mind of the Spirit, because the Spirit intercedes for the saints according to the will of God" (Romans 8:26–27, RSV).

I love how those verses acknowledge that we don't always know how to pray. I find that very reassuring. Don't you? But did you also notice that verse 26 highlights the truth that we "ought" to pray? As the poet has put it, "Prayer is the Christian's native breath." In other words, if you need to breathe, you need to pray.

But just as our breathing can become shallow or labored in times of weakness or stress, so it is with our praying. We are weak, we labor in prayer, sometimes we feel like our prayers are shallow, and often we can't catch our spiritual breath. But the Holy Spirit accepts our small, feeble, human offerings and takes them to the throne as deep, eternal, and appropriate sacrifices. He transforms our shallowness into worthy requests before the Father because He knows the deep things of God. Amazing.

That's why you can still pray even when you can't (or think you can't).

That's why you can still pray even when you don't feel like it, and don't seem to have a single worthwhile word to say to God.

That's why you can still pray even if you don't have confidence in your ability to pray. It doesn't matter. You *can* have confidence in the ability and faithfulness of the Holy Spirit to interpret your prayers.

So, pray. It is the true mark of a Christian.

THE MARK

Making good time down the Damascus Highway, Paul eagerly anticipated his next opportunities to hunt down and persecute followers of "the Way." Known as Saul the Pharisee at that point, he had rightfully earned a reputation as the most dreaded and brutal oppressor of the newly formed Christian faith.

But Saul's travel plans were interrupted. It wasn't a flat tire on his chariot or road construction and flaggers by the Syrian Department of Highways. Saul was stopped short—knocked flat, to be precise—by a sudden encounter with "the Light." Literally blinded, he was led by the hand into the city, where he awaited the further instructions Jesus told him to expect.

In the meantime, the Spirit of God spoke to a believer named Ananias, saying, "Go to the house of Judas on Straight Street and ask for a man from Tarsus named Saul, for he is praying" (Acts 9:11). God gave Ananias a distinct clue about the spiritual condition of Saul, the persecutor. He pointed out only a single quality and action as living proof of Saul's conversion. God simply said, "He is praying." The

New Living Translation version translates those words, *"He is praying to me right now."*

I love that. That is the mark of a true believer. God didn't acknowledge *how* Saul was praying. He just told the reluctant Ananias that the man who used to persecute followers of Jesus was now praying to Jesus.

I doubt that Paul's prayer was worthy of canonization at that point. It may not have been eloquent or even very coherent. He had to have been shaken to the core. Just think, he was now praying to the very Name he had scorned, hated, and tried to wipe off the map. In his distress, he may have prayed the simple psalms he'd memorized as a child at synagogue. He may have knelt there in his new blindness, saying over and over again, "I'm so sorry, Lord, I'm so sorry. I didn't know...I didn't know."

He may have prayed the simple prayers of a child or of a traveler who has lost his way in the wilderness. But don't miss the profound point: *He prayed.* I'll bet he prayed like crazy. I know I would have. Paul's simple act of praying became the visible evidence of his changed heart. We don't have any record of those prayers, but God does.

And that's what matters to God. That's all God wants: our sincere prayer. It doesn't matter whether we're on our knees, stretched out facedown on the carpet, or sitting in a car; whether our hands are folded in reverence or soaked in dishwater. All that matters is that we learn to pray. And in so doing...we learn to fall.

WE ALL FALL DOWN

I remember a busy Wednesday morning that commenced a "fall-down day." I opened my eyes that morning and felt the weight and worries of the day descend on me before I could even get out of bed. My schedule was packed: errands, responsibilities, back-to-back appointments, and a constantly chirping cell phone consumed every moment.

As the minutes passed, so did any assurance that I was going to pull off all the demands of the day. By 9 a.m. I had greeted my assistant, paid the garage door repairman, and taken phone calls from the preschool, church, and my husband.

And then...*I fell down.*

But that was a good thing.

In fact, I even fell with two other people—at the same time. I often fall alone, but on that day, I needed someone to fall with. So down in my basement, before I left for my first appointment, I grabbed Dotty and Tammy (the housekeepers who sneaked in behind the garage door repairman) and announced, "Put down your mops, girls. We need to pray."

You see, when I speak of "falling," I am talking about laying it all out before our Father. To me, falling means that I bow in my heart, falling before Him in weakness and worship. I've learned that "When I bow to God, God stoops to me."[29] So when I fall, I then rise in joy and strength and I'm able to walk on. In fact, the Bible recommends these "group falls." James 5:16 says that we should "pray for one another," and Matthew 18:20 reminds us that where two or three are gathered in His name, He is there also.

On that particular morning I'd felt my need for God's strength so keenly that I knelt in the hallway, holding hands with Dotty and Tammy. Maybe in some cathedral somewhere at that moment, some priest in embroidered vestments was kneeling before an altar with fragrant incense wafting through the air. But down there in my basement hallway with the housekeepers, it was the scent of Clorox and Pine-Sol that filled the room. And we fell down together in our hearts as we stood in a circle of unity. I thanked them and my Father and then left the house.

On the way to my first appointment, Katie, my assistant, told me about her husband's job dilemma. "Jennifer," she suddenly interjected, "we need another fall. You pray while I drive." After I said a concluding "Amen," she said, "Well, Jennifer, I think this is Fall with Your Friends and Family Day.'" We chuckled as we parked in front of the hair salon.

After I shed some burdens and a whole lot of extra hair with my precious stylist, Paulette, she teared up as she told me about her latest heartache. Again, I grasped her hands and we fell. In the middle of a busy salon, on a busy day, we met together with Jesus. We gave Him our weakness, and He gave us His strength.

The day continued, and so did the falling. A man named John, my neighbor Lori, my husband, and an entire staff from a Christian publisher via conference call were eventually added to the Falling Friends and Family roster.

Have you had one of those fall-down days lately? Sometimes we may be reluctant to fall with others because we're intimidated or embarrassed. But when we catch a glimpse of our profound need for God and our need for each other, we become willing to risk embarrassment in order to receive strength.

Besides, it's not just for ourselves and our own needs that we fall with our friends. No, we fall for the sake of others, too. We share in their weakness and join them in their search for strength and guidance. Prayer ushers each of us before the very throne of God Himself, and in that place, we are changed.

If you want to keep running your race with endurance, fall to your knees on that race track and connect with your heavenly Father. So many of us fool ourselves into thinking we'll get more done and go farther if we keep running, running, and running all day long. But in the Christian life, falling down gets you further in the race than running.

If you want to walk by faith, always choose to fall. Fall down for your needs. Fall down for the needs of others. Fall down in repentance over sin. Fall down in reverence. Fall down in thanksgiving and praise. If you need to fall alone, do so. But never forget the power and joy of a group fall. And as you fall, you'll find your burdens falling, too, because "the LORD upholds all those who fall and lifts up all who are bowed down" (Psalm 145:14).

It's really true: God does lift up those who fall down. Peter said, "Humble yourselves, therefore, under God's mighty hand, that he may lift you up in due time" (1 Peter 5:6). I've felt that lifting-up hand again and again in my life. I've even noticed some fellow fallers in the pages of God's Word.

A WHOLE LOT OF
FALLING GOIN' ON

I decided to see how some of my spiritual predecessors prayed and what they prayed about. And what do you think I found? A whole lot of falling going on.

We spoke about Paul earlier. Suddenly curious to know how he prayed and what he prayed, I began searching through his New Testament letters. In so doing, I learned a lot about the purpose of prayer. Check this out.

Paul asked the church in Rome to pray that he would be able to come for a visit, that he would be rescued from unbelievers in Judea, and that his service in Jerusalem would be acceptable to the saints.[30]

He asked the Corinthian believers to pray that he would be rescued from deadly peril.[31]

He asked the church in Ephesus to pray that he would fearlessly advance the Good News.[32]

He called on the believers in Colosse to ask God to open a door of ministry for him, and that he would be able to proclaim the gospel clearly.[33]

He asked the Thessalonian church to pray that the message of Christ would spread rapidly, and that he and his companions would be delivered.[34]

The writer of the book of Hebrews asked the Jewish believers to pray that he would lead an honorable life, and that he would be restored to them.[35]

Here's what I find fascinating. These "falling" letter writers didn't ask for comfort, luxury, or self-gratifying conditions to prevail. If you review again what you just read, you'll see their requests falling into four categories:

- Future fellowship
- Favor from God
- Clear and fearless proclamation of the message
- Furtherance of the gospel

What a model for us to follow. Their prayers weren't self-centered; they were God-centered. When our prayers are merely self-centered, they lead us to a self-centered faith. In other words, a dead end. But if our prayer requests are God-centered, they direct us toward God. This kind of God-centered faith doesn't run out of steam and quit when the road grows long.

God-centered praying focuses our attention on His purposes. Notice how often the apostles requested prayer for themselves. And with each request, they sought to fulfill God's plans and desires. Praying for yourself, then, is not necessarily self-centered. As your desire becomes God-centered, so will your praying. And that's a way to thrive.

Consider with me, how many of your requests fall into the category of seeking God's favor? How about fearless proclamation or fellowship? Or what about furthering the gospel message in your neighborhood, your city, and out across the world? I have considered these things—and it's made a difference in the way I pray, and in the way I ask for prayer from others.

And guess what? That kind of New Testament praying

is infectious. It sets an example for all who pray *with* you.

We need each other. We need someone to fall with. But sometimes our prayers for others seem a little shallow and surface-y—like a simple recitation of their latest wants and needs. How do you pray for your loved ones more deeply?

Fortunately for us, the New Testament writers recorded more than just their requests for prayer. They also wrote down the actual prayers they offered up for others. So let's see what happened when they fell for others. You'll love this.

Paul prayed that the Corinthian brothers and sisters *would grow in maturity.*[36]

For the believers in Ephesus, he asked the Lord that *the eyes of their hearts would be enlightened*, so they could better understand their hope and their inheritance in Christ. Pleading with God for these saints, Paul asked that *they would be strengthened in their inner man*, and that *Christ would dwell in their hearts through faith.* He prayed that *they would have power to grasp the love of God,* and that *they would be filled to the measure of the fullness of God.*[37]

For the Philippians he prayed that *their love would abound in depth and insight.*[38]

And for the Colossian believers, Paul got really cranked up. He asked God that *they would be filled with the knowledge of God's will and have spiritual wisdom.* He prayed that *they would live a worthy life, bear fruit, and grow in the knowledge of God.*[39]

Opening his heart to heaven on behalf of the young church at Thessalonica, the apostle prayed that *they would be supplied with all they lacked, that God would count them worthy, and fulfill their every good purpose and act of faith.*[40]

For his Ephesian friend, Philemon, Paul prayed *that God would help him actively share his faith so he would have a full understanding of every good thing we have in Christ.*[41]

Do those prayers sound like the prayers you pray for your friends and family...your children...your spouse? Do you pray for their growth and maturity and their enlightenment to see spiritual things? Do you pray that they will have strength in their innermost being or that they would be filled with the knowledge of God's will? Do you petition God that they would have spiritual wisdom and live a worthy life?

SWIMMING FOR THE DEEP END

As I reviewed these prayers of Paul and others, I didn't see anything about Demetrius getting a better job, or Hannah finding "Mr. Right," or Apollos getting along with his mother-in-law, or Lydia finding relief from her arthritis, or Gaius passing his chariot driver's exam. Now there's nothing *wrong* with any of those requests. God cares about what we care about, and He's interested in every detail of our lives.

But these prayers of the apostles made me think about going deeper in my petitions for others. Too often I ask God for superficial things, either for myself or others. I splash around in the shallow end of my prayer life, but God invites me to dive into the deep end.

Oh yes, we know that we ought to pray. The apostle James reminds us that "you do not have because you do not ask" (James 4:2, NKJV). Too often we go without simply because we neglect to bring our requests to God. We are stuck within our spiritual poverty, our loneliness, and even live without blessing just because we don't pray.

God meets our deepest needs through prayer, but even more magnificently, *He* meets us in prayer. Prayer allows us to cooperate with the work He's doing in us, and it offers a rendezvous through which we can know Him.

Prayer isn't meant to be intimidating; it's supposed to be inviting. But there are times when life is just simply too big, too complex, too overwhelming, and we don't know what to say or what to ask for. That's when I remind myself that even though I may be overwhelmed, the Holy Spirit is not. He can take my wordless longings, my unnamed fears, and my jumbled thoughts and weave them into a lovely, seamless intercession before the Father.

Those life-is-too-big moments are also times when I choose to "trade places."

"TRADING PLACES" PRAYER

Sometimes, when I pray, I can't see the forest for the trees. My prayers sound more like gibberish than well-thought-out petitions. Drowning in the sea of my own problems, I feel like I'm flailing and grasping, tossed by the waves, never able to clutch the life preserver just beyond my reach.

That's when I shift my prayers to someone else.

And what a difference. I can see *their* forest and *their* trees with perfect clarity. I can lean over the edge of my boat and toss a life preserver into their reach with exacting precision.

I remember unloading my frustrations on my friend Karen while we talked on the phone one day. Sometimes blindness just scrapes against the bottom of my soul and makes me tired, and it was one of those days. My thoughts were fragmented, and I was so overwhelmed by circumstances that I could barely articulate my heart.

Then it was Karen's turn. She poured out her concerns about her mother's recent diagnosis of cancer. Like me, she was so overwhelmed that her thoughts had become patchy, and she could barely make sense with her words.

And then Karen hit upon the solution. "I know!" she said. "I'll pray for you today, and you pray for me. I can handle praying for your situation much better than I can figure out how to pray for mine."

I was struck by the intuitive wisdom of her suggestion. Sometimes I just get worn out in my prayers. Subjectivity skews my ability to petition wisely. Yet objectivity brings a great advantage to prayer. My deep love and concern for my friend Karen caused me to seek God diligently on her behalf. Because I was a spectator I was able to see her playing field more clearly.

Of course God wants us to seek Him for our own needs. He says so time and again. But to show that kind of persistence on someone else's behalf invites God's power to overwhelm them. And catch this—His power splashes over into our own lives, our own situations. As we become a channel of His grace, mercy, kindness, wisdom, and provision, God lets that channel overflow the banks, flooding our own lives.

On that day of "trading places" prayer, I didn't feel empowered because my own circumstances had changed. Somehow, God's grace and power swept through me as I poured myself out for Karen. Paul said as much to his friends in Corinth. "For we rejoice when we ourselves are weak but you are strong; this we also pray for, that you be made complete" (2 Corinthians 13:9, NASB).

Sometimes I feel God's presence most mightily when I am freed from the shackles of self. It is empowering to carry another's burden to the throne. When we do, it strengthens our spiritual muscles and invigorates our spiritual stamina.

We are stronger and sturdier because of our persistent pleas before the throne of grace. Left to myself and my own needs, I become weary and hopeless. But praying for someone else emboldens me and gives hope and confidence that my own needs will be met. "Prayer always works. But beware: through it God may work upon us in ways we would never have anticipated."[42]

Oh my friend, bearing another's burden will certainly lighten your own load. "Carry each other's burdens, and in this way you will fulfill the law of Christ" (Galatians 6:2).

If you're getting worn out or feeling intimidated or powerless in your prayers, maybe you should trade places or fall down with your friends and family. You can certainly experiment by imitating the way the early apostles prayed. But most important...just pray. Pray for others, pray with others, pray by yourself and for yourself. But keep on praying and never stop.

Corrie ten Boom summed it all up by asking, "Is prayer your

steering wheel or your spare tire?" God just wants to hear from you. He loves you and longs for you to call upon Him so He can direct your every step. It is your life's breath to pray, so *breathe*.

"Pray to Me," our God tells us, "and I will listen to you" (Jeremiah 29:12, NASB).

What could be intimidating about that?

CHAPTER NINE

Hold Onto Hope

Hope was as elusive to me as a black leather watchband with a silver clasp.

Okay, I know that might sound strange to you. But after three exhausting hours of searching, I was starting to lose hope.

I had just purchased a new Braille watch that I was crazy about. It was silver rimmed with a midnight-blue face. The only problem was that its black leather band was too big. So I set out to get it adjusted. My pilgrimage began at a likely place to fix a watch—the jewelry counter at the largest department store in the mall.

A nice older gentleman offered to help me while I waited. As I handed him my watch, he fumbled, and his hands shook as he tried to hold it in his grasp. *Oh no*, I thought, *this is not going to work out well.*

I was right. An hour later, I was still standing there.

Finally, the aged salesman handed my watch back to me in its original condition, regretfully informing me I would need another band—and his store didn't have one that would fit.

So my friend Pat and I left the store and ambled through the mall. We popped into a jewelry store and asked if they sold black leather bands with silver clasps. "None here," a disinterested clerk mumbled. (If you're not there to buy diamonds, you're definitely a second-class customer.)

In the next jewelry store we encountered, the salesman examined my watch and told me he thought it was fixable.

"No way," a gruff female voice interrupted. "Can't be done." That's when I was introduced to the other sales-woman. Ignoring his comrade, the first salesman still held out hope. "But you will have to wait thirty minutes for my manager to return," he said.

Pat and I decided to get some lunch while we waited for the manager. After grabbing a quick bite in the food court, I was armed with a better attitude, better blood sugar levels, and renewed hope. We returned to the jewelry store and found seven customers ahead of us in line for service.

When she saw us, the crude-sounding saleswoman who had discouraged me earlier yelped, "The manager isn't back yet."

"We can't wait," I replied. Just as we turned to leave...the manager arrived. *Hope at last!*

The salesman explained my situation. I could feel waves of irritation radiating from the manager's person. He stretched and twisted my watch, peered at it, unbuckled it, and then went behind the counter. "Can't be adjusted and can't be replaced" was his pronouncement. "You should go to the leather repair shop. Maybe they can cut it down."

At this point, my desperation was growing and my optimism was shrinking. The parade of watch experts was not amusing me any longer. I was glad I was with my friend Pat, who was a fairly new Christian. It made me more mindful of guarding my tongue and testimony.

So, with fading optimism and growing frustration, we trooped into the leather repair shop. By that time, I had my speech down, and handed the repairman my troublesome timepiece.

Still barely hanging onto hope, I waited for him to emerge from the back with a well-fitting watch. But it wasn't to be. Instead, he held out the watch and exclaimed, "I'm not touching this." Pat gasped at the now dangling buckle which the repairman had broken. He said it would have broken anyway and there was nothing he could do.

"Take it back to the jeweler," he suggested.

Without responding to him, I slung my cane out in front of me and turned toward the door. I didn't even risk holding him responsible for the broken clasp since I was so irritated. Pat's view of godliness might have been compromised by my verbal explosion. Now my favorite watch wasn't even wearable.

We searched out the last jewelry store in the mall in hopes of finding a new band. And again, no black bands with silver clasps were available. Finally the Zales salesman told us to try the department store around the corner. "I think they have bands," he said.

"You think? Or you know?" I pressed.

"I know."

"Okay, Pat," I sighed. "Let's try one last time." So we entered the department store and found the watchbands. Pat told the salesgirl, who sounded like she was about twelve, that we needed a black band with a silver buckle, size 14. The girl rifled through a basket with Pat's help, occasionally giggling and pulling out bands one by one. The scenario went something like this:

Girl:	Here's a cute one!
Pat:	Yes, but it's a size 16.
Girl:	Oh. Here's another one. It's to die for!
Pat:	It's a size 12.
Girl:	Oh, well. I love this one!
Pat:	It's a size 16 also.
Girl:	(*Giggles*) I don't really know what those numbers mean!

I am intentionally omitting my own thoughts from this exchange. You don't need to know those. It wouldn't be good for my reputation. Let's just say, I stayed quiet...and tried to hold onto *hope*.

I finally bought the only black size 14 watchband with a silver clasp in the store. It was on clearance and cost three dollars. It was plastic and very tacky, but at least I could wear my watch.

I asked if the salesgirl could please attach it to my watch. "No," she responded, "I don't know how. You should try the Watch Doctor."

"The who?"

"The Watch Doctor. He's at that little kiosk just outside the entrance."

By the time I arrived at the Watch Doctor's clinic with my oh-so-tacky band, I had lost all sense of decorum. I was spent, and not nearly so concerned about Pat's opinion of my testimony anymore. And so, like a crazed, worn-out, hopeless woman, I whined loudly and all in one breath, "Help me! I just need a new band, or an adjustment on my old one, or at least I need this tacky one attached to my watch. No one can help me. It's taken three hours and nothing is working."

Somewhere in my hapless account I must have mentioned the watch was Braille. "Braille?" the good doctor gasped. "Are you blind?"

"Yes," I answered.

"Can I pray for you?"

"Yes," I moaned, "but sir, I really want you to fix my watch first."

"What can I pray for?" he asked as if I'd never mentioned the watch.

He took out a pen and paper, ready to write. "What's your name?" he asked. I told him my name, introduced him to Pat, and learned that his name was Rick. As gently as I could manage, I relaxed and tried to refocus him on the watch. He asked me if I knew Jesus.

"Yes," I replied. "Know Him and love Him."

"Hallelujah!" he shouted. "I love people who love my Lord!"

"Me, too," I said. But what I was thinking was, *Now,*

brother, fix the watch. We talked about Christ and our salvation as he and Pat tried to find a new band. When Pat found the perfect one, she lamented, "But it has a gold buckle, and we need a silver one."

"No problem," the doctor smiled. "I'll just switch it. Only take a minute." No one else during the earlier watch wars had even hinted that such a maneuver was possible. But Rick just kept raising the praise and working on the watch. He was my brother, and he was making sure that his sister's watch was just right.

When he finished, I paid him and buckled the watch. He then grasped my hands, and there, in the middle of the mall, Rick prayed for me. And I thanked God for my newly discovered brother. I told him how he was my last hope and that he redeemed the whole day for me, and he just laughed as if he knew exactly what I meant.

In Romans 5:5, Paul tells us that hope will not disappoint us. What the apostle doesn't say in that verse, however, is that hope may take you down some interesting paths. Hope most certainly will require perseverance, but it will also help you remain focused on the prize.

HOPE HOLDS YOU

We must hold onto hope. But if you are weary, you can allow hope to hold onto you.

Phil and I celebrated our nineteenth wedding anniversary on August 9 of this year. He was actually only nineteen years old when we met, and now he's been my husband half his life.

On his dresser sits a beloved picture that was taken outside of our college dining hall just a few months after we began dating.

In the photo, I have long, straight black hair with thick bangs. He has bushy, curly, blond hair. We are both in faded jeans and tennis shoes. I know exactly what we were wearing even without seeing the picture because I remember when the photo was shot. He and I were walking hand in hand, and when our friend with the camera yelled, "Smile!" Phil dropped my hand, put his arm around me, and grinned.

Now, almost twenty years later, Phil still holds my hand. Or, is it that I still hold his? Who is really holding whose? Hmmm.

When our youngest son Connor walks with me or his dad, he too reaches for a hand. He quickly places his small hand into our larger ones. He snuggles; we grasp. Even if Connor were to let go, he would still be held within our grasp. Again, who is holding whom?

To me, simple hand-holding is a lot like hope. It seems like we hold onto it, but really hope holds onto us. Since I first found faith in Christ, hope has held me and I have held onto the hope that holds me.

So if that's the case, what helps us hold on as we are being held? What keeps our little hand clinging within the larger hand of hope? According to Romans 15:4, it's two distinct things...perseverance and the encouragement of Scripture.

> For whatever was written in earlier times was written
> for our instruction, so that through perseverance and

the encouragement of the Scriptures we might have hope. (NASB)

Think for a moment how amazing this is. We have in our possession a book that is thousands of years old—and it is as relevant to life in the twenty-first century as this morning's newspaper or today's page in your date book. Why should an ancient book assembled by a diverse group of prophets, farmers, shepherds, kings, fishermen, and minor government officials offer any hope to men and women in the grip of contemporary problems, pressures, and heartaches?

Because God Himself put that Book together, that's why. It's a book that is not only relevant, it is *alive.*

For the word of God is living and powerful, and sharper than any two-edged sword, piercing even to the division of soul and spirit, and of joints and marrow, and is a discerner of the thoughts and intents of the heart. (Hebrews 4:12, NKJV)

How can a book be alive? Because God spoke it, God continually works through it, and God's Spirit shines the light of understanding on its pages, for those who seek Him and His ways. The hope that touches the lives of those who read it, then, is not some shallow, surface-y, will-o'-the-wisp, wish-upon-a-star kind of hope, but a *living hope.* A hope that can reach anywhere, and to anyone. A hope that can overcome anything.

The words penned in Paul's day are the very source of encouragement and hope for us today. In fact, how fabulous that every lesson we learn in the Light leads us to greater perseverance and ultimate hope.

PERSEVERANCE

The New Living Translation phrases Romans 15:4 this way: "Such things were written in the Scriptures long ago to teach us. They give us hope and encouragement as we wait patiently for God's promises."

To "wait patiently" is to lay a steady, patient hand to the plow...even if the plow seems to be idle at the moment.

That's perseverance. It reminds me of the only kind of exercise I actually enjoy. It's called isometric contraction. You can do it while you wait in a long grocery line or while you're stuck in traffic. You can engage in it while you watch TV, or while you wash dishes.

Maybe you've tried it before. It's where you flex and firm your muscles even when you are supposedly still. It's actively participating in strengthening yourself even when you're not moving. It's a great picture of perseverance.

Moses set this example for us:

By faith Moses, when he had grown up, refused to be known as the son of Pharaoh's daughter. He chose to be mistreated along with the people of God rather than to enjoy the pleasures of sin for a short time. He regarded disgrace for the sake of Christ as of greater value than the treasures of Egypt, because he was looking ahead to his reward. By faith he left Egypt, not fearing the king's anger; he persevered because he saw him who is invisible. (Hebrews 11:24–27)

Perseverance is how we cling within the grasp of God. It's waiting, not pulling back prematurely; it's staying and standing even without visible results. That kind of trusting tenacity leads us to a hopeful expectation. Perseverance leads to hope in the same way quitting leads to feelings of hopelessness. When we give in or give up, we eventually give out.

The word *perseverance* in Romans 15:4 shows that the phrase "holding onto hope" is quite accurate: It is an unwavering unwillingness to let go and give up. As Tertullian said, "Hope is patience with the lamp lit." Is your lamp lit today, my friend?

Speaking of lamps, I have learned the tough lesson of perseverance from living with no physical light at all—the difficult, unrelenting teacher of blindness. There are times when I just want to quit. What is a small task to a sighted person can be an enormous feat for me. Walking to my mailbox, navigating unfamiliar restrooms in airports, negotiating different stages in different venues and cities every time I speak, and hundreds of other small and big challenges can really wear me out.

To be honest, my fatigue often exceeds my fortitude. It would be easier to just draw the lines a little closer to home, keep my world smaller, simpler. Venturing out of my "control zone" takes a lot of energy, and sometimes I have to give myself a pep talk to keep marching on.

But this I know—and I hope with all my heart I can explain it to you.

The hopelessness I feel when I give in to my blindness is far more debilitating than the fatigue I may feel from persevering through it.

Here's what I mean. There have been many a morning that I have gotten my boys off to school and husband off to work just to go straight back to my room and crawl right back into bed. Feeling overwhelmed, discouraged, I pull the covers over my head and try to disappear. When I give in to the temptation to give up like that, I find myself slipping toward the cliff edge of depression and despair. At least when I cry my way through hard days, at least when I forge on through my frustrations and keep on keeping on though I am discouraged and weary, my perseverance serves to strengthen my hope.

When I give up, I begin to relinquish hope. When I stop persevering, it's like I loosen my grip within the greater hand of hope. It's only when I keep clinging, grasping, and am unwilling to quit that I truly feel hope holding onto me.

We all feel the weight of hopelessness from time to time. I know you have felt it. Maybe you are feeling it right now. The Light offers constant pep talks that help us to persevere. In fact, the writer of Hebrews offered encouragement to the worn-out believers who were beginning to lose their grip on hope.

If you've ever felt yourself walking on that cliff edge of despair, sit yourself down and read the book of Hebrews. Read it in a modern translation or a paraphrase or whatever version you like—just open its pages and ask God's Spirit to stir you and speak to you in the deep places of your spirit. He will! That's precisely why the book of Hebrews was written. And God had *you* in mind even as it was being penned.

It was originally penned to a generation of believers who were experiencing the heat and pressure and heartbreak of unrelenting persecution. Some of them were on the verge of giving up, turning back to their old religion and their old ways. Knowing this, the writer poured out his heart, pleading with these discouraged men and women to remember those who had gone before them, and to keep their eyes on the greatest of all prizes, the Lord Jesus Himself.

Hope is strengthened by endurance and is eroded by quitting. So my friend, keep holding on, persevering, enduring. But don't forget the second thing Paul mentions that helps us hold onto hope...the encouragement of Scripture.

HOW SCRIPTURE ENCOURAGES

The Word of God can encourage you when you are discouraged. It can offer hope when you feel hopeless. It can shed light when your world is dark. God knows we need hope, and He provides the encouragement of His Word to remind us that we are held by an extraordinary hope.

Read His Word. Cling to it. Hold it so close to your own heart that you can hear the heartbeat of God in its pages. It will fill you with hope as it works in your heart.

And so, looking with you to the encouragement of Scripture, let me remind you of the hope which holds you.

Your hope is in God.

> Blessed is he whose help is the God of Jacob,
> whose hope is in the LORD his God....
> The LORD is good to those whose hope is in him,
> to the one who seeks him.
> (Psalm 146:5; Lamentations 3:25)

Your hope is not in yourself or in your ability to fix all of your problems. Your hope is not in your spouse or your romantic interest. Your hope is not found in your boss's reaction to your work or your children's acknowledgment of your worth. Your hope is not in church membership, religious rituals, or "keeping all the rules." Your hope is not in any other person, place, or institution in your life.

It is in God and God alone.

Hope in anything other than God Himself will always disappoint.

The psalmist understood these things very well. "Lord, where do I put my hope? My only hope is in you" (Psalm 39:7, NLT). When our hope is in God alone, not in what God can do for us, then we will not be shaken. Place your hope in Him and you will never be disappointed (Psalm 71:5).

Your hope is in the power and majesty of His Name.

> And his name will be the hope
> of all the world....
> I will praise you forever for what you have done;

in your name I will hope, for your name is good.
I will praise you in the presence of your saints.
(Matthew 12:21, NLT; Psalm 52:9)

Your hope is not in your own power and ability. Your hope is not in any influential relationships or associations you might have. Your hope is not in whom you know or who knows you. Your hope is not secured by or found in any authority except Christ. Your hope is profoundly and singularly in the powerful Name of Christ and in His majesty alone.

You can be joyful in hope.

Be joyful in hope, patient in affliction, faithful in prayer.
(Romans 12:12)

You can't always be joyful in your circumstances. You can't find joy in wishing, worrying, or wondering. But you *can* be joyful in hope, because it is a sure thing. It will never let you down. Hope never promotes sorrow or despair, and that's why you can be joyful.

Hope holds the seeds of faith and love.

We have heard of your faith in Christ Jesus and of the love you have for all the saints—the faith and love that spring from the hope that is stored up for you in heaven and that you have already heard about in the word of truth. (Colossians 1:4–5)

Hope does not promote lies or ill will. Hope will never deceive you or lead you into malice, ill will, or outright hatred. Hope is the incubator that nurtures your growing love and fortifies your belief in God's truth.

Hope is the foundation for faith and knowledge.

> ...a faith and knowledge resting on the hop.e of eternal life, which God, who does not lie, promised before the beginning of time. (Titus 1:2)

Hope is a sure bedrock upon which you can build your faith life. It is not a foundation of shifting sand; it is steady. It is not subject to cracks and compromise, so you can erect a fortress of truth and knowledge upon it with confidence. Hope will remain a secure rock even when all around you is shifting sand. It is a resting place for your trust and understanding.

Hope is your calling.

> I pray also that the eyes of your heart may be enlightened in order that you may know the hope to which he has called you, the riches of his glorious inheritance in the saints, and his incomparably great power for us who believe. (Ephesians 1:18–19)

You are not called to despair, throw in the towel, and quit. You are called and equipped to choose hope. It is your invitation to a neverending party where water is turned into wine. You are called to and destined to believe, persevere, and thrive regardless of your situation. Despair is not your calling. Negativity is not your calling. Pessimism is not your calling. Hope is. Cling to your calling, and feel your calling cling to you.

Hope is a gift from God.

> "For I know the plans I have for you," declares the
> LORD, "plans to prosper you and not to harm you,
> plans to give you hope and a future." (Jeremiah 29:11)

You can't earn hope, like a salesperson racking up points for a company award. You can't manufacture hope through frenzied activities or dedication to some tried-and-true formula. You can't maneuver yourself into the path of hope, so that it somehow overtakes you because you're in the right place at the right time.

In fact, hope is a gift. A gift from God Himself. He gives us each hope, and it's up to you and me to unwrap the gift. Make hope your own. He gave it to you so you would use and enjoy it.

Hope will never disappoint you.

> And hope does not disappoint us, because God has
> poured out his love into our hearts by the Holy
> Spirit, whom he has given us. (Romans 5:5)

People will disappoint you. Loyalty fails, relationships change, friends drift away. Places where we have lived and loved and created happy memories change into places that feel strange and no longer like home. Someone cuts down the old trees or tears down the old, familiar buildings. Or blight sets in on a once lovely neighborhood, stealing its warmth and charm. Health disappoints us. We don't feel the way we'd love to feel, sleep the way we wish we could sleep, or heal from sickness and wounds the way we long to heal. Plans disappoint us. No matter how we dream and plan, things don't always turn out the way we expect. We can't control factors that can change everything in an instant. Sometimes all our strategizing crumbles before our eyes.

Disappointment is part of our fallen world, but hope will never disappoint us when our hope is from God and in God's Word. Say with the psalmist, "You are my refuge and my shield; I have put my hope in your word" (Psalm 119:114).

Hope is the anchor for your soul.

> This hope we have as an anchor of the soul, a hope both sure and steadfast. (Hebrews 6:19, NASB)

Hope grounds you and ties you to that which is immovable. Instead of being tossed about by the winds of circumstance, you will become welded so that you can never be shifted, transplanted, or dislodged.

Hope will embolden you.

> Since we have such a hope, we are very bold.
> (2 Corinthians 3:12, ESV)

Hope gives you guts. Boldness way beyond your own. It prompts you to act with the courage God has granted you. Despair cowers in the corner of disappointment, but hope makes you the brave believer God intended. Hope causes you to have the courage to claim God's promises and the bravery to believe revelation even when reason abandons you. Hope lets you shout optimism when others whisper dark words of cynicism and despair.

Hope is alive.

> Praise be to the God and Father of our Lord Jesus Christ! In his great mercy he has given us new birth into a living hope through the resurrection of Jesus Christ from the dead. (1 Peter 1:3)

Hope lives on, even if all your dreams blow away on the wind. When the widow of Zarephath made her last meal and then prepared to die, hope's cupboard was still full.

When Hannah cried out of her own barrenness, hope was ready and waiting to conceive.

When the lame man was lying beside the pool of Bethesda, hope was preparing his walking shoes.

When Naaman's flesh was being consumed by leprosy, the river of hope was able to cleanse.

When Gideon was afraid, hope was posturing for victory.

When Paul was thrown in prison for preaching, hope refused to be silent and spoke truth to the guards.

When the prophet Jeremiah cried tears of sorrow and disappointment, hope was his only comfort.

When Elisha's servant felt alone against the enemy, hope was the army that protected the prophet he served.

When David felt vulnerable, hope gave him security and refuge.

When Jesus' body lay lifeless in the tomb, hope was resurrection waiting to happen.

Hope is Jesus Himself.

> Paul, an apostle of Christ Jesus according to the commandment of God our Savior, and of Christ Jesus, who is our hope... (1 Timothy 1:1, NASB)

Hope is not a philosophy or a theory. Hope is not a personality trait or a quirk. Hope is not a concept or a dream. Hope is a person. Hope is Jesus. And the most amazing part is that hope is Christ in you (Colossians 1:27). Other men see only a hopeless end, but the Christian rejoices in an endless hope.

Wow—what a hope. Hold onto it as it holds onto you. Don't fix your hope on earthly things like financial security, unruffled relationships, or restored health. The temporary things can never be a true source of hope. Instead, fix your hope on God and His eternal Word.

A week from now...a year from now...a million ages from now...you will not be disappointed.

CHAPTER TEN

Be God Conscious

A few years ago I was invited to a special dinner sponsored by a publishing house. As a rookie author, I was excited beyond measure. The evening held such a promise of joy that I began early that afternoon to get ready for the big night—trying on several dresses, and working harder than usual on my hair.

When I was fully groomed, I couldn't decide which earrings would provide the nicest finishing touch, so I placed a lovely and very dramatic silver earring in my left ear and then secured a graceful, more modest hoop in my right. I figured when Phil returned to the hotel he could help me decide which looked best.

But when Phil arrived, it was obvious he was *not* as excited as me about the dinner. Instead of preparing hours in advance, he burst into our hotel room five minutes before we were to leave. Trousers flew, shirts whisked straight from the suitcase onto his body, cologne splattered, and his hair was given a quick once-over.

Then he breathlessly announced, "We're gonna be late!"

Caught up in this chaos, I grabbed his tie and raced to the door, completely forgetting about my own appearance.

Despite Hurricane Phil, the Category Four who had just blown through my tranquil world, I was still excited. Nothing was going to ruin my evening. Brimming with anticipation, I entered the restaurant on my husband's arm, and we were shown to our seats.

To my delight, I found myself seated between a notable editor and a well-known chef. Our conversation was lively and captivating. I laughed, listened, learned, and loved every minute of it. I was conscious of nothing but the nuances of the moment. This was pure joy, and I allowed myself to simply be caught up in the wonder of the experience.

After descending from my cloud and floating back into our hotel room, Phil warily inquired, "Um, Jennifer, did you *mean* to wear two different earrings?"

"Oh, nooo!" I shrieked. "How *embarrassing!*"

I quickly became self-conscious, imagining how foolish I must have looked with my wildly mismatched earrings. I wondered what the folks at dinner must have thought of my fashion faux pas. They probably stared. Or snickered. Or at least did a double take.

Frankly, the thought began to ruin my evening...in retrospect. I hadn't been self-conscious for a moment during dinner. I was too swept along in the joy and pleasure of the occasion, the engaging people I had met, and the goodness of my God to even think much about myself.

But now...the more I recalled the experience, the more painfully self-aware and humiliated I felt. My great joy simply evaporated.

That's what self-consciousness does. It steals our joy. It deprives us of the prospect of living beyond ourselves. It places the magnifying glass of excessive scrutiny on us, enlarging our little mistakes and shortcomings completely beyond measure.

By contrast, God-consciousness continually preserves joy, keeping us fueled and focused on our faith journey.

When our awareness of God exceeds our self-awareness, we are positioned to thrive—even when things in our lives (like my earrings) don't match up.

THE NEVERENDING DANCE

It's a hard balance to strike...a healthy self-awareness and self-love coupled with a greater God-awareness and love for God.

You know what I mean. That tension between thinking about God and thinking about yourself is a constant struggle. But it shouldn't be a wrestling match or race to see which one wins.

Think of it more like a dance.

Think of it as a cooperative, step-by-step interplay

between us and God. He leads, we follow. We move to the rhythm of grace and truth that helps us to strike the perfect balance.

Here's how we can do it so our joy will really be complete. Think of yourself as a dwelling place—the place where the glory of God dwells. Here's the way Paul put it:

> Do you not know that you are a temple of God and that the Spirit of God dwells in you?... Or do you not know that your body is a temple of the Holy Spirit who is in you, whom you have from God, and that you are not your own? (1 Corinthians 3:16; 6:19, NASB)

God intended for us to have an awareness that He dwells in and with us. But because God dwells in the temple of our bodies and our personalities, we must also maintain a healthy self-awareness.

Self-consciousness is appropriate, as it directs us to good stewardship and management of our personal temple. The temple itself isn't the object of worship; it is the One housed in that temple who deserves our devotion and attention.

Stick with me for a moment while I take this thought just a step further. Paul told the Thessalonians there would come a day when the "man of lawlessness" or the "anti-Christ" would set himself up to receive the attention and worship that only Jesus deserves.

Paul describes the enemy of Christ as he "who opposes and exalts himself above every so-called god or object of worship, so that he takes his seat in the temple of God, displaying himself as being God" (2 Thessalonians 2:4, NASB).

Even though it's a radical picture, it reminds me of what I do in my own spirit of selfishness. In the temple God has given me, the place where He is to be enthroned, I set up my own throne, built brick by brick with the glue and mortar of self-awareness, self-consciousness, self-preservation, self-protection, and even self-promotion.

There is one temple, and only One in the temple worthy of worship.

And it's not me.

Imagine for a moment that your job was keeper of the Temple in ancient Israel. Every morning you wake before dawn to enter the Temple courts with your broom and your mop. All throughout the day—and until the last worshiper departs, rejoicing through the front doors at night—you occupy yourself with dusting, arranging, cleaning, oiling hinges, and polishing wood.

Now that's a good occupation, and pleasing to the Lord—if you are doing it just for Him and out of love of Him. But what if you say in your heart, "I don't need to be a part of any of the worship services. I don't need to sing the psalms or raise my hands to God or participate in the offerings. I'll just spend that extra time patching cracks in the plaster or sweeping along the baseboards"?

So as God's people weep and worship and repent before Him, bringing offerings of their best and pouring out their hearts in praise, you're back in one of the storerooms on hands and knees retouching the paint behind the door.

Is God pleased with you? Wouldn't He say to you, "I am pleased you honor My Temple, but the Temple is only a vehicle for approaching Me and connecting with Me. You have turned your back on the main thing—on life itself—to busy yourself with needless minutiae"?

When I am fully self-conscious, not God-conscious, I worship myself, not God. Self-exaltation never leads to joy. It only leads to further self-scrutiny—and then more painful self-awareness.

The Temple was erected to be a dwelling place for the presence of God. So is the temple of our lives. As David wrote, "In Your presence is fullness of joy" (Psalm 16:11, NKJV). Joy is a result of God-consciousness, not self-consciousness.

MIRROR, MIRROR, OFF THE WALL

To have that kind of view of myself, I must look in the one true mirror. I must pray like the psalmist, "Turn my heart toward your statutes and not toward selfish gain" (Psalm 119:36). Yes, to be more God-conscious than self-conscious, we must recognize that we are the temple dwelling of God, but we must also look into the mirror of God's Word.

Dwight L. Moody once said, "We ought to see the face of God every morning before we see the face of man."

The first face you see each day will greatly influence who occupies your thoughts throughout the day. When you look into your bathroom mirror, you see your face. But to see the face of God, you must look into the mirror of His Word.

In fact, the apostle James compares God's Word to a

mirror. He tells us that looking into God's mirror and applying what we see brings blessing. "But one who looks intently at the perfect law, the law of liberty, and abides by it, not having become a forgetful hearer but an effectual doer, this man will be blessed in what he does" (James 1:25, NASB).

If you've heard me speak before, you've probably heard me tell stories about mixing up my makeup. Yes, I have on occasion mixed up my eye liner and lip liners because I couldn't see into a mirror to behold the strange distortion I was creating.

Because the story of my makeup mishap is familiar to so many, I completely blew off the constructive criticism that Lucy Swindoll offered me one evening right before I went onstage at a Women Of Faith conference.

"Your eyes don't match," she said flatly.

"Very funny," I retorted. I was sure she was trying to capitalize on my story—or maybe just trying to keep me relaxed before I spoke.

But Lucy was serious. "No," she insisted, "really, one is black, and one is brown."

"That's impossible!" I replied. That funny and mischievous Lucy was not going to get the best of me on this one.

"Jennifer, I am *serious*," she said with as much maternal authority as possible. "Ask Nicole."

So I turned to Nicole Johnson, the talented dramatist on the Women of Faith team. But before I could ask, she gasped, "She's right. One is black and one is brown."

I opened my makeup bag and sure enough, I had two different eyeliner pencils. One black, one brown. (Note to the visually impaired reader: Never carry two different shades of eyeliner in the same makeup bag.)

It is true: I have not been able to see into a mirror since I was fifteen and lost the majority of my sight. Of course, even though I joke about my many mishaps, I still wish I could see myself. I would love to be able to look into a mirror to see what I look like. I would much prefer to choose my own hairstyle or blush color. And yes, eyeliner. What woman wouldn't?

But even though that reality is frustrating, it causes my eyes to gravitate to a mirror that I *can* see. In fact, the mirror I look into now shows me exactly what I look like, exactly who I am.

It is the mirror of God's Word.

My blind eyes can see 20/20 as I gaze into its light. I may not see my physical image in the bathroom mirror, but in God's mirror, I can see that I am created in God's image. I know from Ephesians 2:10 that I am the very workmanship of Creator God.

The mirror of God's Word helps us see ourselves and our God in a way that promotes a healthy balance between our God-consciousness and our self-awareness. Have you looked in that mirror lately? Gaining God's perspective on who we are allows us to find a healthy balance. It keeps us from an inflated or deflated view of ourselves and allows us to assess ourselves in the light of God-consciousness.

The mirror in your bathrooms—even clear of steam— doesn't reflect truth. It is at the mercy of your perspective and your interpretation. We know very well there are some attractive people out there who look into a mirror and see only ugliness. What is happening in that instance? They are looking, but they are not *seeing*.

Physical mirrors can't reflect truth; they only offer optical illusion. Only the mirror of God's Word reflects truth, because it *is* truth. It grants you a right perspective of yourself as it reveals a true view of your Father.

But don't just look at the mirror; look *into* it. Gaze long and hard, the way you do when you are applying eye shadow or fixing your hair. The way a man does when he is shaving around those small creases and tiny lines.

"The Bible is like a telescope," Philip Brooks wrote. "If a man looks *through* his telescope, then he sees the worlds beyond; but if he looks *at* his telescope, then he does not see anything but that. The Bible is a thing to be looked through, to see that which is beyond; but most people only look at it; and so they see only the dead letter."

He's right. How much we miss if we only give the Word a passing glance. Look into it, gaze, and feed on it like Jeremiah, and you will experience the same joy he wrote about. "When your words came, I ate them; they were my joy and my heart's delight, for I bear your name, O LORD God Almighty" (Jeremiah 15:16).

"OPEN THE EYES OF MY HEART, LORD"

Our gaze into the mirror of God's Word is intended ultimately to reveal God, to allow us to see Him, and therefore heighten our awareness of Him. It is incredibly powerful. Powerful enough to actually alter what we see, and change our perspectives. No matter what we are experiencing, no matter which page we set our gaze upon, the Light is able to reveal realities we weren't even aware of.

My friend Marcey recently sent me an e-mail that reminded me of the sheer power of God's Word to shape our thoughts and perspective. Just for a moment, take a peek into my e-mail Inbox for an excerpt of her letter.

Dear Jennifer,

I just realized today how we (or maybe it's just me) have become such "topical" Christians. For instance, if I'm going through "divers temptations," there is an instantaneous feeling that I need to be spending all of my time in James. But right now, Scott and I are completing this 6-week study in Genesis on Abraham; I am working through a 28-day book on prayer and also preparing a Sunday school lesson each week. (Let alone sneaking peeks at the *Strong-Willed Child* book.) Who has time to expand to James and take care of three children, a husband, and a house?

My point being, after completing the prayer study and the study on Abraham during Neeley's morning nap, guess what I found? Peace! Order to my chaos! Absolute joy! Have we, as Christians, slowly slipped into a pattern of thinking that says, "In order to benefit from God's Word, we must find the Scripture that speaks specifically to our current circumstances or 'topic'"?

Wow, did I underestimate the power of God's Word or what? Obviously, you can learn anything from God's Word at any time, anywhere in the test. But over the past two days of studying Abraham, I have learned that He is *El Roi*, the God Who Sees; He is *El Shaddai*, the All-Sufficient One; He is *Adonai*, Lord and Master. And the understatement of the year is that I have grown and I have been blessed!

Your friend,

Marcey

Marcey's right. The Light is incredibly powerful to open our eyes, tenderize our view, focus us, and allow us to really see. If you are struggling with a level of self-consciousness that debilitates you and blinds you to really seeing your Father, then keep looking into the mirror.

I have experienced firsthand the power of God's Word to open eyes. I never cease to be overwhelmed at the comments I receive after I speak. Women will recite detailed accounts of how God spoke to them through His Word while I taught.

The amazing thing is that more often than not, what they heard is not what I said. God's Word speaks for itself and is always personal, applicable, and precise.

And it will always lead to unspeakable joy.

Do you want your joy to be full? I sure do. Learn this lesson shown to us in the Light. Remember that the source of joy is not found in us but in God. When you allow yourself to be full of God instead of full of yourself, you will be satisfied by the sweet fruit of joy.

Joy is from God (Psalm 16:11).
Joy is a promise (Psalm 30:5).
Joy is a mindset (James 1:2–3).
Joy is your strength (Nehemiah 8:10).
Joy is your inheritance (Isaiah 61:7).

Look into His mirror, my friend, and you will see who you are and who He is. As you see yourself, recognize that you are a temple, the place where almighty God chooses to make His dwelling.

Does He wear you well?

CHAPTER ELEVEN

Enjoy the Fishbowl

I was a typical new parent when my son Clayton made his entrance into the world. Everything our little guy did was duly noted and recorded in the pages of his baby book—and discussed in happy detail with all my friends who were new moms. Phil and I could go on and on talking about what a bright and delightful little man the Lord had given us.

So you can imagine the excitement in our apartment on the day Clayton spoke his first discernible word.

"Ball."

Yes, that was it.

Soon after that great verbal breakthrough, other words followed. Within days he added words like "up" and "juice" and "Dada." I was growing in anticipation with each new word, especially when "Dada" was added to Clayton's growing vocabulary.

The addition of "Dada" surely meant that the much coveted "Mama" was on the horizon, and I couldn't wait to hear it. After all, it seemed as though I had been pregnant for years...and I now had stretch marks in places I didn't even know were stretchable. I felt like it was only right that I should be rewarded for giving this little boy life by hearing his sweet voice lift up a tender "Mama."

But it didn't come.

Oh, he continued to add words, but "Mama" wasn't one of them. Frankly, I was growing jealous. It just didn't seem fair. Clayton constantly uttered his Daddy's name. "Dada, juice," he would say. Or he would beckon from his crib, "Dada, up." I don't think I was completely unreasonable in feeling slighted. It was his "Mama," not his "Dada," who had gone through labor. Shouldn't there be some reward?

It's not like Phil held it over me, either (he's too wise for that). Still, I couldn't help but think he sounded just a little bit smug when Clayton went on with his "Dada this" and "Dada that."

Well, I could either get upset over being unacknowledged by the apple of my eye, or I could just relax, stop stewing about it, and enjoy being a new mom.

I decided on the latter course. And as my jealousy cleared, so did my judgment. In fact, I began to notice an interesting pattern emerging in Clayton's vocabulary. *He was calling me a name.* It wasn't the name I was expecting to hear, so it took some time for me to notice. No, he wasn't calling me "Mama."

He was calling me *"God."*

I kid you not. If Clayton wanted juice from his daddy, he would call out, "Dada, juice peas!" But if he wanted me to get his juice, he would call out, *"God,* juice peas!"

Somewhere in the forming of his verbal repertoire, he inserted the name he chose to call his mother, and it was none other than God. (Now it was my turn to refrain from being smug.)

As a first-time mom, I, of course, called the pediatrician to make sure this was not a problem. He counseled that it was just probably easier for Clayton to say God than Mama, and I was not to worry. Besides, I could be called a lot worse. It's just that Phil and I couldn't figure out how Clayton had come to this conclusion. Phil, though he treated me with love and respect, certainly didn't refer to me as deity.

After contemplating the matter, the only reason I could come up with was this. Clayton would see me in the kitchen, preparing food for dinner, then we would sit at the dinner table and pray, "Thank You, God, for our food."

I guess Clayton just assumed that since I was the one who made the food, and we thanked God for the food...I must be God.

Whew! That's a lot of pressure—and I didn't want to start getting used to the title. I was grateful when, at thirteen months old, Clayton started calling me "Mommy."

Have you ever heard anyone call you God? Probably not, but that doesn't mean that others aren't thinking it.

There are people in your world who look at your life and

wonder, "Who is God, anyway?" If they know that you walk in the Light, they will undoubtedly look to you to discern what God is like.

They might not even do so consciously or deliberately. You may never be aware that you're being observed. But if you are known to believe in and belong to God, there will be those who are watching, wondering. *Is God patient? Is He kind? Is He consistent? Does He really care?* Recognizing that others watch our lives as a billboard advertisement for what God is like helps us take seriously all the lessons we learn in the Light.

Some of us like the challenge of such a predicament, but others of us might feel a tinge of pressure. It's like living in a fishbowl.

A PLACE TO SHINE

Sometimes I feel like I live in a fishbowl. My life is on display, every move noticed, every choice laid open for analysis. Let's face it. You don't have to be in public ministry to struggle with "fishbowl" feelings and issues. Your faith life puts you on display. The light within you shines in the darkness of this world, and people notice it.

But don't worry. Your fishbowl is not a place of pressure. It's a place of privilege.

A fishbowl is an opportunity for others to see God in you. It need not be perceived as a burden, but rather a blessing. A place to shine.

Fishbowls come in all shapes and sizes. They're not just pulpits and brightly lit stages. No, they can be kitchen sinks, carpool lanes, office cubicles, backyard fences, dinner tables, grocery store lines or shopping malls. In fact, a fishbowl is anyplace where your life is observed by others.

And if in fact you do find yourself in a position where you are noticed and observed, don't imagine that you climbed up to that place of prominence and visibility on your own. God lovingly placed you there so that you will reflect Him.

My son Clayton gave me a special gift many years ago, purchased out of his tender seven-year-old heart and his meager budget. It's a small ceramic turtle. It may or may not be artistic—that doesn't matter to me. The little turtle's worth doesn't lie in its aesthetic qualities. It was a spontaneous gift of love from my boy, and it is very precious to me.

The turtle rests within the ring section of my jewelry box. I don't leave it there because I want to hide it; I intentionally placed it there so that every morning when I feel for my rings, I will feel the little turtle.

Clayton chose the turtle for me because he remembered the story I once told him about the "turtle on the fence post." Have you heard of him? He sits proudly upon a tall fence post. He is in a place of prominence where everyone can see and admire him. The interesting thing, however, is that he didn't get there by himself. Someone had to place him there.

I'm like that turtle on a fence post...and so are you.

It's kind of like a fish swimming contentedly in a bowl. How did he get there? He didn't swim upstream to get there. He didn't arrive there by escaping the talons of an eagle. Chances are he wasn't born there.

A fish lives in a bowl because someone put him there. And once the bowl becomes his whole world, he is dependent on the person who placed him there.

Whatever you have "achieved" in life is precisely what you have *received* in life. So... "Don't hide your light under a basket! Instead, put it on a stand and let it shine for all. In the same way, let your good deeds shine out for all to see, so that everyone will praise your heavenly Father" (Matthew 5:15–16, NLT).

The transparent walls within which you swim are a place for you to shine, a place for you to reflect the One who placed you there. There is one problem, however. You won't show who God is if you are distracted by the three perils of fishbowl living.

Peril #1: Pride

Sometimes our fishbowls get cloudy. The pH (pride/humility) balance isn't quite right.

That's what happened to Shebna, the royal treasurer and manager of King Hezekiah's house (Isaiah 22:15). Shebna must have had boundless ambition and great skill to hold two such powerful and important kingdom posts. And though he may have been a capable man, neglect and corruption characterized his work ethic. He was more concerned with pomp, profit, and self-promotion than he was with the wealth of the palace or the welfare of the people.

Shebna's personal pride was no secret among the citizens— nor did it go unnoticed by God. How could it have, since Shebna erected a tomb as large as his pride and as ornate and pompous as his opinion of himself?

Here was a man who was determined to remain the center of attention, visible to all even after his death. God told the prophet Isaiah to confront Shebna. Here's the way Eugene Peterson paraphrases the Scripture:

> The Master, GOD-of-the-Angel-Armies, spoke: "Come. Go to this steward, Shebna, who is in charge of all the king's affairs, and tell him: What's going on here? You're an outsider here and yet you act like you own the place, make a big, fancy tomb for yourself where everyone can see it, making sure everyone will think you're important." (Isaiah 22:15–16, *The Message*)

Shebna set up a fishbowl that was beyond compare. It wasn't enough for him to ride about the city in a magnificent chariot pulled by a prancing stallion. No, Shebna was concerned about his posterity. It bothered him to think that he might be forgotten or overlooked after he departed life. Would history remember his greatness and glory?

With that question burning in his mind, he set out to build a suitable monument to himself. He set it up on high so all could see and marvel. Matthew Henry had it right when he wrote: "Those that make stately monuments for their pride forget that, how beautiful soever they appear outwardly, within *they are full of dead men's bones.*"

High places, for all their view and prominence, are extremely slippery places to stand. The writer of Proverbs rightly warns that pride comes before a fall (Proverbs 16:18). And that's just what happened to this haughty, self-absorbed royal official. Isaiah tells the end of the story.

"Yes, I will drive you out of office," says the LORD. "I will pull you down from your high position. And then I will call my servant Eliakim son of Hilkiah to replace you. He will have your royal robes, your title, and your authority. And he will be a father to the people of Jerusalem and Judah. I will give him the key to the house of David—the highest position in the royal court. He will open doors, and no one will be able to shut them; he will close doors, and no one will be able to open them." (Isaiah 22:19–22, NLT)

Shebna was displaced, disgraced, utterly debased, and eventually replaced. Perhaps the Assyrians captured him and took him away, or maybe King Hezekiah finally got wise to his steward's pride and treachery, and banished him. We don't know for sure. But what we do know is that God caused him to spend his remaining days in obscurity. I think it's a safe bet to assume that Shebna was buried in an unmarked grave. And if his name is remembered at all these days, he is remembered as a fool.

Pride is a legitimate risk of fishbowl living, but it is avoidable. Shebna was accused of being a "disgrace to [his] master's house" because he sought to gain glory from the position he held, stealing honor from the king himself.

And so it is with us. Our great King, the King of kings,

has placed you where you are, and your life should reflect His good character and bring Him glory. Remember that you are a steward, not the owner. Set your aspirations high by taking a low position. Serve the King and serve others with joy and a sincere heart. Don't let your fishbowl become a tomb. Instead, let it be a wellspring of life.

Peril #2: Performance

Because fishbowls have invisible walls, we can become distracted by curious onlookers. We might be intimidated by the audience and feel the need to perform. The praise of man becomes stimulating and we find that we enjoy the limelight.

But limelight is sour when you get a mouthful.

I'll bet that's how King Sennacherib felt.

He lived in a colossal fishbowl of his own making. As ruler of western Asia, he had celebrity status—more infamous than famous (which suited him just fine). Soon after rising to the throne of Assyria, he built a new royal residence in the capital city of Nineveh and called it "the palace without rival." Through all of his building schemes and military conquests, Sennacherib created an empire which served as a stage upon which he performed. He developed quite the public image as "the king without rival."

Subjugating one powerful nation after another and crushing coalitions of enemy kings, Sennacherib began to believe his own press clippings. Who could oppose him? Who could stop him? It reminds me of the classic line from the old science fiction movies: "Resistance is futile."

And then the great Assyrian juggernaut rolled into Judah,

ruled by godly King Hezekiah. The final act of Sennacherib's drama began as he sent a letter threatening the annihilation of Jerusalem, the city the God of Israel had chosen for His dwelling place:

> "Say to Hezekiah king of Judah: Do not let the god you depend on deceive you when he says, 'Jerusalem will not be handed over to the king of Assyria.' Surely you have heard what the kings of Assyria have done to all the countries, destroying them completely. And will you be delivered? Did the gods of the nations that were destroyed by my forefathers deliver them?" (2 Kings 19:10–12)

This is a classic case of overreaching. Question King Hezekiah's leadership? Fine. Insult King Hezekiah's military strategy? Fair game. But mock King Hezekiah's God? Insult God Most High? Watch out.

As protagonist in his own play, Sennacherib supposed his image to be superior to the Lord's. God responded by sending "the angel of the LORD...[who] put to death a hundred and eighty-five thousand men in the Assyrian camp" (2 Kings 19:35).

One angel. One night. One flick of God's little finger.

Death blew through the Assyrian camp like a cold wind sweeping across the plains of Kansas. And just that quickly, the great Sennacherib removed himself from the world stage. What was left of his army withdrew—*fast*. And a short time later, the final curtain fell when he was slain by his own sons.

In his personal chronicles, Sennacherib bragged that he had shut Hezekiah up in Jerusalem "like a bird in a cage." But the puffed-up performer left out a few important facts...like the utter, overnight devastation of his proud army. I guess those minor details don't quite make bestselling autobiographies or get you on the cover of *Time* as Man of the Year. They certainly didn't line up with his image of superiority and invincibility. Sennacherib thought his great performance would always be remembered, but today we consider him (*if* we consider him) as a has-been—little more than an asterisk in history.

Elvis Presley knew about the hollow life that grows from a performance mentality. In a 1972 press conference prior to his record-breaking Madison Square Garden shows in New York City, he told reporters, "The image is one thing and the human being is another.... It's very hard to live up to an image."

Not only is it hard to live up to an image, it's impossible.

An image is a mere snapshot. It can't possibly capture a genuine persona, and is really nothing more than a facade. It's like veneer. It peels and cracks when the temperature changes, revealing what lies beneath.

Living up to an image is an "outside-in" sort of life that majors on externals. How different from the way our God views life. When even a godly man like the prophet Samuel got caught up in the image game, God stepped in to correct him: "Do not consider his appearance or his height, for I have rejected him. The LORD does not look at the things man looks at. Man looks at the outward appearance, but the LORD looks at the heart" (1 Samuel 16:7).

Performance that comes from a true and devoted heart brings glory to God. Mere external performance that doesn't correspond to the man or woman on the inside is simply playacting...and will eventually be exposed as such.

Peril #3: Problems

When the fishbowl gets jostled, waves ensue. The difficulties of life can make it hard to desire staying so visible. Sometimes we just want to hide, nurse our wounds, or even escape the pressure.

I am so glad that David didn't jump out of the fishbowl and go into hiding after the whole Bathsheba tragedy. Think what you and I would have missed: his repentance and forgiveness...his broken, humbled spirit...his sweet psalms of restoration.

Psalm 32 would never have made it into the Book...

Blessed is he whose transgressions are forgiven,
whose sins are covered.
Blessed is the man
whose sin the LORD does not count against him
and in whose spirit is no deceit. (vv. 1–2)

Psalm 51 would have never comforted us...

Cleanse me with hyssop and I will be clean;
wash me, and I will be whiter than snow. (v. 7)

Psalm 25 would have never helped us turn back to God...

> For the sake of your name, O LORD,
> forgive my iniquity, though it is great. (v. 11)

David knew what it meant to sin deeply and to experience deep forgiveness and overwhelming grace. And what he experienced has become a bright light to our pathway in the darkest of times.

Or what about Paul? What if every time he went on a missionary journey he was haunted by his past as a persecutor of Christians? What if he had never been able to let go of the images of innocent people condemned, becoming racked with guilt and paralyzed by regret? Would we still have the book of Romans—or any of the other epistles that reveal God's great plan and mysteries hidden for generations? How could he have ministered to anyone? He would have drowned in a sea of guilt and condemnation rather than sailing above the tumult of his past.

Instead of hiding, however, Paul humbly accepted the gracious call of God, declaring, "Forgetting what is behind and straining toward what is ahead, I press on toward the goal to win the prize for which God has called me heavenward in Christ Jesus" (Philippians 3:13–14).

Yes, when you're living in the fishbowl, people watch while you try to keep your head above water. It doesn't matter whether you're dealing with a shady past, a shaky present, or a clouded future; pressing trials and traumas and worries should alert us to our own brokenness and draw us to wholeness in God.

I have peered into two prominent fishbowls recently, and that is exactly what I saw...God's wholeness.

As a guest speaker for the national Women of Faith conferences, I am usually seated on the front row next to the other guests. In my first year at the huge conference, I was most often coupled with Sandi Patti and Chonda Pierce. During a conference in Minneapolis, Sandi, Chonda, and I sat in our usual seats.

Chonda is a bestselling author and hilarious comedienne who has saved my husband thousands of dollars in therapy bills—because she makes me laugh all my troubles away. Though she is excruciatingly funny, she is also acquainted with deep pain, having overcome a difficult past and struggles with depression. When she arrived at the Minneapolis conference to do her presentation, it was obvious that a tough battle with her depression had transpired before she got to the arena. She was emotionally worn out when she took her seat next to Sandi.

You probably know Sandi Patti. She's a phenomenal singer who has won Grammy awards, Dove awards, and has tons of blockbuster recordings to her credit. Sandi's world came crashing down about ten years ago when she made some choices that resulted in the demise of her marriage. She, too, is acquainted with deep pain and profound forgiveness.

When we were first introduced, I was struck by their legendary status. But the more time I spent with these women, the more I became impressed by their authenticity. Each knew what it meant to be broken, and each knew what it meant to be restored—rebuilt by God's Spirit from the inside out.

The crowd gave Chonda a thunderous ovation when she took the stage. I prayed for her strength. Sandi cheered and laughed at every joke as if it were the first time she had heard Chonda's routine. Toward the end of her presentation, she transitioned into some serious words. She told the eighteen thousand women gathered in that arena that she understood what it was like to feel alone, to feel hopeless, and to be overwhelmed with problems. She also told them God understood. As she began a song, the crowd was hushed, with the exception of a few sniffles.

As she finished the first verse, a few bars of accompaniment led into the chorus. It was in that moment that I heard something that reminded me why we stay in the fishbowl even when we struggle with problems: Sandi, knowing the lyrics Chonda was about to sing, spoke out with conviction during the hush of the music, "Tell 'em, Chonda!" Just as Sandi spoke those words, Chonda belted out from the bottom of her soul, "God loves you..."

My eyes filled with tears. Sandi Patty wanted the thousands of women gathered in that arena to know what she has learned in her brokenness—that God loves her. Chonda, in her frailty, stood boldly on that stage and proclaimed the same message of hope, the truth that has held her life together when her world fell apart: God loves her.

Sandi and Chonda know the love of God from the bottom of their beings. Because they are willing to stay in the fishbowl, all the onlookers who observe their lives can hear and see the profound message. God loves you...and He makes you whole.

My friend, that's why we stay in the fishbowl even when the water heats up or becomes icy cold. It is in the midst of problems that we taste the refreshing living water. It restores us, cleanses us, and gives us a message to speak.

HOLY FISHBOWL

Did you know that your fishbowl is brimming with living water? That's what Jesus offered to the woman at the well in Sychar. He described this fountain as a "spring of water welling up to eternal life."[43] The Light uses the revitalizing character of water as a symbol to picture the great gift of salvation, leading to eternal life. Water also portrays the indwelling life of the Holy Spirit[44] and the life-giving truth of God's Word.[45]

So, then, life in the fishbowl is really a life spent swimming about in a refreshing spring, a fountain of life. It is from this cascading stream that we receive the cleansing, comfort, and refreshment of the fishbowl life. And we can sum up that life in just one word: holiness.

Holiness had never seemed like a blessing to me; in fact, I had come to think of it as a crushing burden. It seemed so unattainable. It reminded me of constant striving, like swimming upstream. For years when I thought of holiness, I conjured up a picture of a stern, tight-lipped, mean-spirited preachin' woman with her hair in a bun, no makeup, and a long, bony finger scolding the rest of us spiritual peons with "Thou shalt's" and "Thou shalt not's." Not a beautiful picture is it?

Part of the reason for my misguided opinion grew out of a basic misunderstanding of what God told His people in the book of Leviticus. "You shall be holy to me; for I the LORD am holy and have separated you from the peoples, that you should be mine" (Leviticus 20:26, RSV).

God told His chosen people to be holy; now, in Christ, the same command applies to us. Intimidating? To me it used to be. Since I thought I couldn't attain holiness on my own, I would often try to simply "perform" holiness as I swam along in my fishbowl, maintaining all the "do's and don'ts."

The result, I assure you, was forced, artificial, and not attractive at all. I just couldn't see holiness as something lovely and desirable.

But it is. God calls holiness *beautiful*. Scripture speaks of the "beauty of holiness."[46] To understand why God calls it beautiful, you have to look at the original language. The word we translate as holiness derives from the same root from which we get our English word "wholeness." In other words, holiness means "wholeness," or being complete.

Holiness is not intended to evoke images of peculiarity or strangeness. It's supposed to bring to mind a picture of completeness—the whole of God filling the whole of you. To be "whole" or "holy" is to be full of God's completeness, rather than our own brokenness.

What our Father said to His people in Leviticus was essentially, "I want you to be whole as I am whole." That's what He's saying to you and me, too. He wants to fill our brokenness with His wholeness. He is complete, in harmony with Himself, and He wants to replace our emptiness with

His balanced and radiant fullness. Wow! Holiness *is* beautiful. I want it and I need it. Don't you?

We all know what it's like to be broken. We know how it feels to be aware of our incompleteness. But to be whole is to have God take all the pieces of our personalities and our passions and perfectly balance us.

Without holiness, I am not capable of handling my life. In my brokenness, I put up a big facade and try to bluff my way through. It is then that I am most susceptible to the perils of fishbowl living. I puff up with pride to cover my insecurities, I conjure up a performance mentality, or I become overwhelmed with my own problems and just want to bail. Those are symptoms of a lack of wholeness—a deficiency that hurts both myself and others.

WHOLENESS

Some time ago, I was scheduled to be the final speaker at a large women's convention. Prior to my presentation, Beth Moore dazzled and inspired the thousands of women gathered in the arena. The worship had been skillfully and tenderly led by Travis Cotrell. Everything about the weekend had gone beautifully, and God was present with us.

When I awoke on Saturday morning, however, I was nervous. It was my turn to speak, and I felt intimidated to follow someone like Beth Moore. I was anxious and painfully self-aware. I prayed and read the Word, but I really felt like a wad of emotions inside.

I went to breakfast that morning with Mandisa

Hundley, a talented and gracious singer and worship leader, who was to lead worship that morning before I spoke. She, like me, was far less well-known than Beth and Travis.

And so, with Jennifer being full of Jennifer instead of God, I opened my mouth and began to speak. It went something like this: "Mandisa, I sure hope they give you and me a good introduction, since no one knows who we are." I continued on with more unnerving and unnecessary comments. Believe me, I feel a wave of embarrassment even as I write about this. I did not say anything ugly or sinful. I just didn't say anything that built up Mandisa or the potential of our ministry together. I said nothing that promoted wholeness in Mandisa and everything that exposed my own brokenness and insecurity.

As I continued, Mandisa grew quiet. Her unresponsiveness was my first clue that the whole of God was not filling the whole of me. Instead, there was a giant hole in me, and I was filling it with junk.

Within moments Mandisa arose, muttered something about brushing her teeth, and quickly excused herself. I sat alone. Well, not totally alone. With me was a growing awareness that I was full of myself, rather than God.

It was in that painful moment that Travis called out, "Hey, Jennifer. Do you want me to walk you to the green room?" I tried to keep my composure as we walked, but inside I was crumbling. The empty hole that could have been filled with God was acting as a vacuum and sucking the life out of me.

When we finally got into the green room, there sat

Mandisa. Evidently, Travis could tell by her wet eyes and dripping mascara that she had been crying. Without even seeing her, I could tell, too. As soon as the door closed behind us, I also burst into tears.

Now, at this point, I wish I could have seen Travis. Two women sobbing, for no apparent reason...and there he was—standing in the green room amidst the emotion and estrogen. I'll bet his silent prayer at that very moment was, "God, remind me once again that You have called me to work with a bunch of women."

While Travis was praying and possibly pondering his future in ministry, I maneuvered my way to the couch where Mandisa sat and said, my voice frail from my own emptiness, "I'm so sorry. I was wrong and I'm so sorry." She consoled me and I consoled her. (I don't know if anyone was consoling poor, bewildered Travis.)

All three of us prayed, and by the time she went out on stage, Mandisa seemed intact. As she began to minister, her holiness was obvious. I sat backstage and prayed and cried. My lack of holiness had hurt Mandisa—and could have damaged her ability to minister.

It hurt me, too. And God. I fought the shame, compelling myself to stand on the promise that God had forgiven me and cleansed me by the washing of His Word.

And then it was my turn to step out under the lights.

At least I wasn't struggling with pride or a performance mentality as I stepped into that vulnerable fishbowl moment. In fact, I had difficulty simply maintaining my composure. Honestly, it was one of the hardest messages I've ever presented. All I really wanted to say to that eager crowd of women was, "God was gracious to me. Mandisa is my hero. And I am desperate for God. If He doesn't fill me, I will fill myself—and the result is ugly. I need the whole of God to fill the whole of me. (And, by the way, please pray for Travis. I'm afraid I scared him out of the ministry.)"

Holiness is neither complicated nor self-propelled. It's not the sum of all the thou-shalts and thou-shalt-nots. It's not merely the absence of sin.

It's the absence of self.

The Pharisees in Jesus' day may have had a lack of sin—at least from their own narrow reading of the Law. But they had no lack of self. Jesus said of them, "You hypocrites! Isaiah was right when he prophesied about you: 'These people honor me with their lips, but their hearts are far from me. They worship me in vain; their teachings are but rules taught by men'" (Matthew 15:7–9).

When we live a Spirit-filled life, leaning hard on our Father, immersed in living water within our fishbowl, then His holiness will find expression through our lives. A radiant, lovely wholeness will wrap itself around us like a living fragrance.

My beloved pastor, John Marshall, often reminds us that "holiness matters most." He's right. It does matter most. Without it, we can neither enjoy nor reflect our heavenly Father.

Oh, my friend, let the Light within you shine.

As you enjoy life in a fishbowl, I encourage you to draw life from the living water and let it sustain you, grow you, nurture you, and fill you. Your purpose in the fishbowl is not to perform, but rather to reflect the One who placed you there. He is the one who chose you, and He is the one who will feed you, care for you, and empower you to thrive.

If you find yourself wanting to complain about a fishbowl life constantly observed by others, just remember that if you're filled up with God, they won't see you anyway.

Looking right through your brokenness, they will see the Lord in all His wholeness, tranquillity, and radiant beauty.

And that's why He put you in the fishbowl to begin with.

CHAPTER TWELVE

Live Like an Alien

When I was a little girl, my parents were missionaries near San Jose, Costa Rica. Our house in San Pedro Sula had a tin roof—designed to lessen the effects of an earthquake. Our front door opened directly to the sidewalk, eliminating any chance for a front yard. The small backyard was surrounded by a wall topped with pieces of broken glass to discourage would-be robbers from scaling it. Small windows were located high off the ground, again to deter thieves.

The only vulnerable window was a small jalousie window that opened onto the carport. Although we didn't own a car, the Catholic priest in the barrio parked his car there, and we'd leave the light on at night to protect his vehicle.

Word must have gotten around that some rich gringos lived in the house across from the church. As missionaries, we really had very little, and the house had been furnished by another missionary family home on furlough. Our borrowed home, however, was one of the few that had a car in the carport. So it was assumed we were rolling in the dough.

One night, my dad got up during the wee hours to check on my little brother. The house was still and silent as he walked to Lawson's bedroom. But just as he returned to his own room, he heard a sound coming from the dining room. As he got closer, he realized that someone was removing the jalousie window panels, one by one, between the carport and the dining room.

Dad's mind raced. He was keenly aware that he was a noncitizen and had to be very careful how he proceeded. He knew he couldn't use a weapon, and yet—what if the intruders were armed? How was he to protect his family?

My dad prayed silently, and a plan came to mind. It had to work, he reasoned, because he didn't have time to come up with another one. Slipping back into Lawson's room, he grabbed a rubber Halloween mask. It was grotesque—putrid green with eerily oversized eyes and electrified hair. Crouching beneath the curtains, he slipped on the mask, counting until the thieves were on the last window panel. As they pulled it out, a dark hand reached through the curtains.

Just then my masked father shot up, jerked the curtains open, and screamed at the top of his lungs.

Two young Latino thugs leaped backward with such force

that they dented the priest's car and broke the glass panels stacked at their feet. One made the sign of the cross and shrieked, *"Dios mio! Dios mio!"*

After that, word must have gotten out that the gringos weren't to be messed with...because we never were again.

During those years, we were sojourners in a foreign country. We remained American citizens even though we lived in Costa Rica, and we were always mindful that this was not home.

But really...who could ever forget that fact?

The living conditions and food, not to mention the language, were all different from our native land. Our cultural dispositions always reminded us that we were resident aliens.

RESIDENT ALIENS

Have you ever felt like you were living with aliens...in your own home?

I couldn't help but wonder that after an encounter in my fourteen-year-old son's room one Wednesday night.

"Clayton," I said, "since your violin concert is tomorrow night, we need to clean and press your uniform." Clayton dutifully rose from his computer and removed his embroidered shirt from the closet.

"It's clean," he shrugged. "No wrinkles."

"Now, what about your black pants?"

"I don't have any."

"What do you mean you don't have any? You wore them two weeks ago."

"Well, yeah, but—they're way too small. The waist is too tight, and when I sit, they come all the way up to my knees."

"Son, you know you need to *tell* me when your pants don't fit. Now there's no time to buy new ones before the concert. You've known for two weeks that the concert was tomorrow. You'll just have to wear the small ones."

Suddenly, Clayton hit on a brainstorm. "I know what I'll do, Mom. I'll just wear Dad's pants."

Now, Clayton and his dad have probably worn the same size at one time in their lives—but never at the *same* time. I was certain that Phil's pants would be entirely too big.

Even so, we rifled through his dad's closet and grabbed some black pants. I insisted he try them on, and was a little surprised to note that the length was perfect. Unfortunately, that was all that was perfect. The waist was huge.

"Oh, Clayton," I said, "they're much too big."

"They look great, Mom. It'll be okay."

He hung the supersized pants with his shirt and went back to his computer. I, on the other hand, was confused and agitated. The battle of the britches had gone silent, but a quiet voice began to sound in my mind. *A daughter would never dream of putting on a pair of slacks three sizes too big for her. Why doesn't it bother Clayton? Should I buy him new pants? This is going to be embarrassing for him...for me...for the entire Dockers clothing brand. Oh well, learning responsibility is more important than wearing well-fitting pants.*

So when concert time arrived on Thursday night, my husband, Droopy Drawers, and I all headed to the middle school gym. It was teeming with sharply dressed young musicians and proud parents. Minuets and Christmas carols filled the room. Then the conductor announced that the orchestra would play a waltz by Strauss.

How lovely, I thought as I settled into my seat.

Instruments were raised and a sweet melody resonated through the gym. My husband, Phil, gently placed his hand on my back. I found myself relaxing and getting lost in the moment.

But as the bows gently caressed the strings, Phil began to rub my back—in rhythm with the waltz. In fact, as the beautiful piece continued, I noticed that each time the students plucked the strings of their instruments, Phil would poke my back right along with their plucking. An apparently frustrated musician, Phil was playing the *Blue Danube* across my back!

Rub-rub-rub-rub-rub, *poke-poke, poke-poke.*

Just like the night before, I was bewildered and frustrated. I thought, *He's not going to stop. He's going to rub and poke his way through the entire waltz!* As I turned toward him I heard him snicker.

"Phil," I huffed, "we're sitting in the front row!"

He pulled his hand away and chuckled.

That's when it hit me—I live with aliens. One is fourteen and the other is forty, but they cannot be from this planet. (Or maybe it's a women-are-from-Venus, men-are-from-Mars thing.) Both Phil and Clayton seemed unmoved and uninfluenced by cultural norms like well fitting pants and basic concert decorum.

So what's a girl to do? I live in a houseful of aliens—

three males and just one reasonable, sensible female...me.

When I think about it, though, I realize being an alien isn't so bad. Being queen of the manor can be pretty nice sometimes.

In a general sense, being an alien simply means you have no permanent ties to the place you live. And shouldn't that describe us as believers?

When my family lived in Costa Rica, we were not permanent inhabitants. As we live here on earth as believers, our residency is not permanent, either. It reminds me of Augustine's idea of the *civitas peregrina*. It's the thought that you and I are simply passing through. We are resident aliens here on earth. Our true home is what Augustine called the "City of God." But until we are actually home, we live in the "City of Man."

According to 1 Peter 2:11, while on earth we are called pilgrims, strangers (KJV), foreigners (NLT), sojourners (ESV), and aliens (NIV). Most world religions consider "alienation" part of their teachings, but the New Testament is unique in that it actively reminds us of our alien status. The Word encourages us to really understand what it means to be an alien here. In so doing, we discover the key to life in Christ. "To believe in heaven is not to run away from life; it is to run toward it."[47]

CULTURE SHOCK

When we lived in Costa Rica, I remember vividly that my mother warned us against eating certain dishes that were served after church, because many of our precious Latin brothers and sisters left their tamales sitting out in the hot sun during the worship service.

My mom, of course, was concerned that we would get food poisoning. I have no idea if those who partook every Sunday got sick, but I doubt it, because it seemed to be their habit, their custom. But it wasn't our custom to eat meat that sat out for hours, so we stuck close to rice and vegetables. Even though we lived there, we still maintained our habits, not theirs. That's how it is as believers. As aliens, we really aren't conformed to the ways of the world within which we live.

The apostle John writes: "Stop loving this evil world and all that it offers you, for when you love the world, you show that you do not have the love of the Father in you" (1 John 2:15, NLT).

As sojourners, our customs are not those of this world; they're kingdom customs.

When the world tells us to keep a big chip on our shoulders and make our violators pay dearly, our custom is forgiveness.[48] What an alien idea. How odd that must seem to many people outside of Christ.

When the world tells us to "look out for number one" and that "charity begins at home," our custom is sacrificial compassion.[49]

When the world tells us to get all we can, buy now and pay later, and go for the gusto, our custom is wide-open generosity.[50]

When the world tells us to "just do it," our custom is self-discipline.[51]

When the world says you can "have it your way," our custom is altruism and humility.[52]

When the world claims that it is "the real thing," our custom is to fix our eyes on unseen realities.[53]

When the world tells us to say, "I'm worth it," our custom is to say, "He is worthy."[54]

As aliens, we speak our own language—the language of love spoken with words of wisdom.[55]

The world we're passing through has a lengthy list of cultural norms. But who has decided what those norms should be? The normal people? And who are they? The things we call normal are nothing more than the result of faulty measuring sticks used by faulty people. So you and I must be less influenced by the cultural norms of this world. And instead we should "not conform any longer to the pattern of this world, but be transformed by the renewing of [our] mind" (Romans 12:2).

To practice this kind of countercultural living is to conform to the culture of heaven, the country of our real citizenship. But our behavior, language, and cultural norms can make us unwelcome in the world at large, and we might feel the sting of isolation.

EXILED AND UNWELCOME

While in Costa Rica, my parents were students at the Spanish Language Institute in San Jose. Dad and three of his missionary buddies were invited by a Catholic priest in a small village to sell Bibles on a Sunday morning. Although my dad would have gladly given the Bibles away, the priest insisted that they sell them, so that the parishioners would view it as a paid for and therefore prized possession. The missionaries were thrilled to partner with the priest in promoting the Word.

The four of them left one Saturday to travel by train to the village, some four hours away from San Jose. Upon their arrival, they immediately sensed they were unwelcome. They made their way to the local Catholic church, but my dad later told me, "When the priest came to the door, he was extremely shaken that we Americans were in town. We introduced ourselves and told him why we had come. Indignant, he told us it was not by *his* invitation. He said that the priest who invited us was no longer at that parish." He proceeded to tell them that they were not to sell Bibles, and that they were not welcome in that village.

The disappointed men returned to the train station. Then, remembering that there wouldn't be another train until morning, they went to a small hotel—but were not allowed to register. They ventured out to a small café for some dinner, but again they were refused service and asked to leave.

The men realized that word had spread quickly—the Americans were not welcome. "We didn't know what we would do for the night," my dad confessed. But through the providence of God, a local man approached them. He was a Christian also. He told them that there were several other Christians in the village that met together for worship. Although none in this small group could house the four missionaries, they did offer a small, deserted railroad shack they used as a meeting place.

As darkness fell, my dad and his friends found themselves in a cramped and vacant shack furnished with only six wood plank benches that the local believers used for their meetings. Some local Christians had provided some candles, water, and a few pieces of bread for their breakfast.

In those days, of course, there were no cell phones, no e-mail. My dad had never felt so alienated and isolated. They truly were unwelcome foreigners with no access to home.

The missionaries found strength in their fellowship, but sleep did not come easily. "Finally," my dad recalled, "we decided to extinguish the candle and seek some sleep. Peace came as we felt that a God who never slept guarded and protected us. As I recall, the four of us did some singing in the dark. It was so very quiet.

"Within minutes, however, the quiet was broken. We knew something—or someone—was in the shack with us. We hurriedly lit the candle, and there, roaming across the rickety floorboards, were rats—five or six of them weighing four or five pounds each. Well, that was enough sleep!"

The men decided to take turns sleeping. It was a difficult night. They knew they were not welcome, and they feared what might happen to them. The reality of harm was there, not so much from the rats, but from the villagers who resented them as intruders. But as my father put it, their fear of man was replaced by their trust in the promise of their heavenly Guardian.

Through the long night, the men meditated on Scripture. Someone quoted from Psalm 139:

Where can I go from your Spirit? Where can I flee from your presence? If I go up to the heavens, you are there; if I make my bed in the depths, you are there. If I rise on the wings of the dawn, if I settle on the far side of the sea, even there your hand will guide me, your right hand will hold me fast. (Psalm 139:7–10)

These truths became the candle that radiated light into their darkness. A golden sunrise came at last, bringing with it the train that would carry them home. As it arrived, they gave thanks to the Eternal Watchman.

Even when we're away from home, our Father is with us in this foreign land. When we feel the sting of exclusion from the world in which we live, we are assured that we are not alone—that God is with us, just as He was with my dad and his friends in a tiny shack in some nameless village in Central America.

He is with you, and you are never alone. Your heart is His sovereign domain, even in your alienation. He is the local believer who feeds you, gives you lodging, and provides shelter and safety. In the dark, His Word is the candle that gives you light.

And there will come a morning, my friend, a bright and cloudless morning when you feel the earth rumble and hear the distant whistle of an approaching train. You are promised a ride home. You have a ticket. No matter your traveling fatigue, no matter your longing for home, remember that there's a train coming.

Part of the reason we can lose heart and run out of steam as we run our race is because we forget that we're just passing through. We begin to think of our earthbound assignment—

with its attendant fears and hurts and sorrows—as permanent. But it's not true. This world in which we live is not all there is. We are simply sojourners; our true home is our true destination.

"Why should my heart be fixed where my home is not?" someone once asked. "Heaven is my home; God in Christ is all my happiness; and where my treasure is, there my heart should be."[56] The writer of Hebrews reminds us that here we have no lasting city, but we seek the city to come.

Heaven is our home.

I've never been to heaven, but I have been to Starbucks.

Please don't be offended. I have no desire to trivialize the magnificence of heaven. But the Lord knows that the only way we earthbound people can think about eternal realities is through earthly comparisons, inadequate as they may be. The Bible compares the Holy Spirit to wind, the Word of God to a radiant light, and even His own presence to the sheltering wings of some great bird.

And Starbucks? Well, it's just the most blissful, relaxing, and thoroughly enjoyable place on the planet to me.

The Bible says that "eye has not seen and ear has not heard...all that God has prepared" (I Corinthians 2:9, NASB). I just can't imagine how blissful, pleasurable, and magnificent heaven must be. But if I multiply the pleasure of Starbucks by infinity to the power of ten thousand million, then I think I am getting a little glimpse of what it must be like. Here's what I mean.

Heaven is a place of pleasure.

Few things in life are as pleasant to me as a piping hot cup of Starbucks coffee sipped slowly in one of their tiny cafes. In fact, I never really enjoyed coffee until I tasted theirs. I love the fragrance of coffee that permeates every molecule in the store. I love to breathe in its richness and warmth. Even the muted roar of the bean grinder makes me happy.

When I go to Starbucks, I am far removed from my daily reality. I get lost in the atmosphere and am transported to a relaxed place of pure delight. My love for the experience is so intense that I even burn a hazelnut coffee candle in my study when I'm writing, just so I can be reminded of that place I enjoy so much. That may seem silly or obsessive, but it's a little slice of heaven to me.

And little slices are all we're allowed this side of life.

Heaven is the place of ultimate pleasure for those who believe in Christ. It's the place where no tears fall, no sighs escape, and no burdens weigh down our shoulders. It's the place where all things are made new. The Bible tells us:

> "He will wipe every tear from their eyes. There will be no more death or mourning or crying or pain, for the old order of things has passed away." (Revelation 21:4)

Sometimes here on earth, we get a little glimpse that ignites our longing. Sometimes we breathe in a fragrance that wafts through our spirit…a reminder and shadow of what is to come. As C. S. Lewis says, "If I find in myself a desire which no experience in this world can satisfy, the most probable explanation is that I was made for another world." We were made for heaven, where ultimate pleasure is realized.

Heaven is a place of passion.

Did you know that Starbucks serves more than thirty blends of single-origin coffees? I know that little fact because Starbucks is one of my passions.

I also know that the first Starbucks opened in Seattle in 1971 at Pike Place Market, and that it got its name from the first mate in Herman Melville's *Moby-Dick*. Starbucks has coffee houses in thirty-four countries outside the United States, and in October 2004, the Starbucks gift card hit the $1 billion mark for total activations and reloads.

Have I convinced you yet that Starbucks is one of my passions?

When we're passionate about something, we learn about it, think about it, and even long for it. Heaven is one of my passions. It's my ultimate destination, and I want to know more about it, think about it, and long for it. Did you know that...

Heaven serves its fruit twelve times each year in abundance from the Tree of Life. And what's more, the leaves of the trees provide healing for the nations. Main Street is paved with transparent gold. Its high wall contains entrance gates made of single pearls, and the gates will always stand open. Jesus Himself will light the heavenly city, doing away with any need for sun or moon. The new heaven and new earth will be established when our sin-cursed planet passes away. The New Jerusalem will experience the peace that the old one never did, and King Jesus will reign forever on its throne. And when we hit the one-billion-year mark for time spent there, we'll not even take note—for time will be no more.

"We talk about heaven being so far away," said Dwight L. Moody. "It is within speaking distance to those who belong there."

Heaven is more real than all we taste, feel, hear, and see here on earth, and it should be an all-consuming passion. Since this world really isn't our home, there should be a healthy sense of alienation at the heart of all our experiences...even in the fragrant embrace of a Starbucks coffeehouse.

We reside here but we are restless.

We are foreigners with a faraway passion.

We are resident aliens with treasures in heaven.

Heaven is a place of purpose.

Every Friday that I'm not on the road, Karen and I go to Starbucks and work on my latest writing project. As you might expect, we begin by ordering a grande skinny mocha with whipped cream for me, and a grande hot chocolate for her. Then we settle in at a tiny table for a three-hour chat on the finer and deeper things of life. We grapple with all we don't understand, we consider truths, we wonder about apparent inconsistencies, and eventually we end up pondering the enormous love of God. We both marvel at the greatness and goodness of God. When we really try to fathom our amazing Savior, it's incomprehensible—all we can do is praise.

That's what heaven will be—a place of purpose. A place to eternally ponder and praise the goodness and greatness of our God. The most amazing thing is that we will "know" as we are "known" (1 Corinthians 13:12, NASB). That means that all that we ponder here, we will realize there. All that we grapple with here, we will grasp there.

Yet I don't think we ever really will get over the magnificence. As Robert Browning once said, "Things learned on earth, we shall practice in heaven." I believe that we will marvel at our Savior, ponder His great love for us, and praise. Praise quietly, praise loudly. Heaven will be the place in which we worship forever.

If heaven is a place of pleasure, passion, and pondering, then earth is the place of our pilgrimage and preparation. Living on earth is our time and place to:

- Look for our heavenly country.[57]
- Turn our faces toward Zion.[58]
- Keep our eyes on our promised dwelling.[59]
- Rejoice in God's Word as we travel.[60]
- Seek the light of God's direction for our journey.[61]
- Remember that we are not at home in this world.[62]
- Shine as lights in the world.[63]
- Gather our treasure in heaven.[64]

As sojourners, we do long for our pilgrimage to come to a close.

That's why we live with such good cheer. You won't see us drooping our heads or dragging our feet! Cramped conditions here don't get us down. They only remind us of the spacious living conditions ahead. It's what we trust in but don't yet see that keeps us going. Do you suppose a few ruts in the road or rocks in the path are going to stop us? When the time comes, we'll be plenty ready to exchange exile for homecoming. (2 Corinthians 5:6–8, *The Message*)

This earthly life God designed for us includes a holy discontent, a longing for our true home, a lingering awareness that we will never feel fully settled or at home here. As with the psalmist, we inwardly yearn, "Oh, that I had wings like a dove! I would fly away and be at rest" (Psalm 55:6, NASB).

Paul makes our citizenship clear by declaring that when "God raised us up with Christ," He also "seated us with him in the heavenly realms in Christ Jesus" (Ephesians 2:6). God has indeed extended an invitation to us to be with Him in eternity, and He welcomes us in and gives us a seat. And He does so at the same moment that He "raises us up with Christ." While your feet are still here on earth, you are seated in heavenly places.

So, my fellow sojourner, tread lightly on this sod. Let your heart keep longing for heaven. Live in this world, feel its pain, cry its tears, and breathe in its air. Let it ignite a sojourner's longing within you. As C. S. Lewis said, "Aim at heaven and you will get earth thrown in." Ephesians 2:19 echoes, "You are no longer foreigners and aliens, but fellow citizens with God's people and members of God's household."

So, come on in. Coffee's on.

Have a seat, and make yourself at home.

Lighting the Way Home

A friend of mine told me about a conversation he had years ago with a man in Portland, Oregon, who lived on a high hill called Rocky Butte.

At that time, there weren't very many houses on the butte, and at night it was a dark, bulky shadow on the horizon. The man traveled as part of his job and found himself away from home for a few days every week. He described how, when he drove south from Washington state into Oregon, he often crossed the Interstate bridge over the Columbia River at night. Looking off to his left, far in the distance, he would see a tiny pinpoint of yellow light twinkling from the dark bulk of Rocky Butte's northern slope.

His porch light.

And the sight of that tiny gleam in the darkness filled his heart with longing and joy...because it told him he was almost home, almost back in the embrace of his loving family.

That's what God's Word is like for His children on the way Home. This world can be a dark and sorrowful place at times, as we make our way toward heaven and our eternal home in God's presence. There are days (and nights) when the way seems long, and hope begins to die within us. That's when we open the pages of the Word of God, and catch a glimpse of Home...a tiny light twinkling in the darkness.

It reminds us that Jesus is coming soon.

"Behold, I am coming quickly, and My reward is with Me." (Revelation 22:12, NASB)

For in just a very little while, "He who is coming will come and will not delay." (Hebrews 10:37)

We who are still alive and are left will be caught up with together with them in the clouds to meet the Lord in the air. And so we will be with the Lord forever. (1 Thessalonians 4:17)

It reminds us that we have a place and a future in heaven.

...into an inheritance that can never perish, spoil or fade—kept in heaven for you. (1 Peter 1:4)

In my Father's house are many rooms...I am going there to prepare a place for you. (John 14:2)

"Father, I want those you have given me to be with me where I am, and to see my glory." (John 17:24)

Finally, it reminds us that while we still walk through this life, difficult as our path might be, He is with us every step of the way.

I will ask the Father, and he will give you another Counselor to be with you forever—the Spirit of truth. (John 14:16–17)

"Never will I leave you; never will I forsake you." (Hebrews 13:5)

"Surely I am with you always, to the very end of the age." (Matthew 28:20)

Don't lose sight of the Light, my friend.
We'll all be Home before we know it.

Let's Keep in Touch...

Thank you for spending your time learning lessons in the Light with me. I pray God has used these lessons to strengthen, encourage, and challenge you to keep running your race with perseverance.

It would be such a thrill for me to hear from you. Did you know I have a computer that reads my e-mail to me? I can't promise the digital voice will sound like yours, but it does allow me to hear how God is working in your life, and through this book. If you'd like to write me, send an e-mail to:

JR@JenniferRothschild.com

Or better, go to the "contact us" link at:

www.JenniferRothschild.com

While you're there, sign up for my Jennifer Rothschild Friends eNewsletter. It's a great way to keep in touch.

I would love to hear how God has illuminated your path through His Word.

And now, my friend...

Let's pray like the psalmist did:

O send out Your light and Your truth, let them lead me; let them bring me to Your holy hill and to Your dwelling places. (Psalm 43:3, NASB)

Blessings,
Jennifer

NOTES

1. Get more of the context of this amazing story in Genesis 12:1–9.
2. Read the full story in Exodus 2–3.
3. This is a tender, beautiful account worth reading all the way through in 1 Samuel 1.
4. 1 Samuel 17.
5. Hosea 1:2–3.
6. Matthew 4:20.
7. Philemon 12–16.
8. Philippians 2:6–8.
9. Galatians 5:16–18.
10. Malachi 3:10.
11. 2 Peter 1:3.
12. Leviticus 1–9.
13. Genesis 4:3–12; Hebrews 9:22.
14. 2 Samuel 6:3–7.
15. Exodus 33:20.
16. Galatians 3:13.
17. Hebrews 2:9.
18. 2 Corinthians 8:9.
19. Ephesians 2:12.
20. 2 Corinthians 12:9.
21. 1 Peter 1:12.
22. Exodus 34:6; Nehemiah 9:17.
23. John 1:14, 17.
24. Mark 5:15.
25. John 4:25–26.
26. John 8:9–11, 17, 26.
27. John 21:18.

28. Acts 9:5–6.
29. *The Quotable Christian*, Robert Chapman.
30. Romans 1:10; 15:30–31.
31. 2 Corinthians 1:10–11.
32. Ephesians 6:19-20.
33. Colossians 4:3–4.
34. 2 Thessalonians 3:1.
35. Hebrews 13:19.
36. 2 Corinthians 13:7, 9.
37. Ephesians 1:15; 3:16–18.
38. Philippians 1:3–19.
39. Colossians 1:3, 9–10.
40. 1Thessalonians 3:10; 2 Thessalonians 1:11–12.
41. Philemon 6.
42. Betsy Childs, "A Slice of Infinity: Does Prayer Work?" Ravi Zacharias International Ministries, September 27, 2005.
43. John 4:10, 14.
44. John 7:37–39.
45. Ephesians 5:26.
46. 1 Chronicles 16:29; 2 Chronicles 20:21; Psalm 29:2; 96:2.
47. Joseph Blinco.
48. Matthew 6:14; Luke 17:3–4.
49. Ephesians 4:32; Colossians 3:12.
50. Matthew 5:41–42.
51. 1 Peter 1:5–8.
52. Philippians 2:13.
53. 2 Corinthians 4:18.
54. Revelation 4:11; 1 Corinthians 6:20.
55. Ephesians 4:29; Colossians 4:6.
56. Margaret Charlton Baxter.
57. Hebrew 11:16.
58. Jeremiah 50:5.
59. Hebrews 11:13.
60. Psalm 119:54.

61. Psalm 43:3; Jeremiah 50:5.
62. Hebrews 11:9.
63. Philippians 2:15.
64. Matthew 6:19; Luke 12:33; Colossians 3:1–2.

FREE Music CD Special Offer!

Get a FREE* copy of Jennifer Rothschild's popular Walking By Faith CD. This ten song collection includes five original songs written by Jennifer, plus "It is Well with My Soul."

Free offer available only online at:
www.JenniferRothschild.com/lightoffer

Other Great Resources
by Jennifer Rothschild

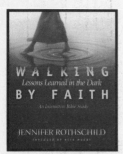

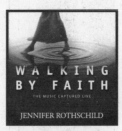

Walking by Faith
Bible Study Member Book

Based on *Lessons I Learned in the Dark*, this workbook features six weeks of interactive material for daily personal study. Includes leader guide.

ISBN 0-6330-9932-5

Walking by Faith
Bible Study Leader Kit

Includes one member book with leader guide and two DVDs that contain seven teaching segments, music videos, and bonus footage.

ISBN 0-6330-9145-6

Walking by Faith
The Music Captured Live

Experience the seven songs you heard during the bible study, plus three additional songs, including a reprise of the traditional hymn, "It is Well with My Soul."

UPC 8-09812-00502-5
Music CD

Walking by Faith
The Music Videos

Enjoy the beauty and gracefulness of the music videos from the *Walking by Faith Bible Study*. Includes family life bonus footage and interviews. On DVD.

UPC 8-09812-00509-4
DVD Video

Along the Way
Songs from the Early Years

You can hear the most requested songs from two of Jennifer's earlier albums, "Out of the Darkness" and "Come to the Morning." If you enjoyed the music from *Walking by Faith*, you'll treasure the music and lyrics Jennifer wrote "along the way."

UPC 8-09812-00492-9
Music CD

Experience God's Touch

RECOGNIZING GOD'S TOUCH ON YOUR LIFE

JENNIFER ROTHSCHILD

Formerly Touched by His Unseen Hand

1-59052-530-2

To a blind person, human touch is essential. In the absence of facial expressions, it reassures and comforts. But can you still feel the warm and soothing touch of an unseen God? Author and musician Jennifer Rothschild, who lost her vision at the age of fifteen, explains how God's touch works from the inside out, warming the heart, mind, and soul. It lifts weights that eyes could never see. It washes away the anguish of guilt, the bite of fear, and the ache of loneliness. With the gentle pressure of His hand on our shoulders, we can find our way through the darkest of nights.

Multnomah® Publishers *Keeping Your Trust…One Book at a Time®*

"We walk by faith, not by sight." 2 Cor. 5:7 (KJV)

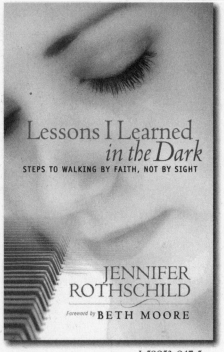

Lessons I Learned in the Dark
STEPS TO WALKING BY FAITH, NOT BY SIGHT

JENNIFER ROTHSCHILD

Foreword by BETH MOORE

1-59052-047-5

At the age of fifteen, Jennifer Rothschild confronted two unshakable realities: Blindness is inevitable...and God is enough. Now this popular author, speaker, and recording artist offers poignant lessons that illuminate a path to freedom and fulfillment. With warmth, humor, and insight, Jennifer shares the guiding principles she walks by—and shows you how to walk forward by faith into God's marvelous light.